GREY OWL AND THE BEAVER

Grey Owl with a Beaver Kitten

GREY OWL AND THE BEAVER

by
HARPER CORY
Fellow of the Canadian Geographical Society

With an account of beaver activities
by
GREY OWL
written for
The National Parks of Canada
and reprinted by their permission

THOMAS NELSON AND SONS LTD
London Edinburgh Paris
Toronto New York

First published, October 1935
Second edition, revised, November 1935
Reprinted, November 1935

H. 118

FOREWORD

GREY OWL is deservedly known as the friend and protector of Beaver, but his world-wide fame is merited above all by the way in which he has impressed people with the significance of the conservation of valuable wild life. Conservation is hampered by the indifference of the general public, by customs arising out of the lengthy exploitation of fur-bearing animals, and, as a direct consequence, by the mistrust of man shown by wild creatures. Therefore, in telling this story, I have included brief accounts of the fur-trade and the problems of conservation, these forming the necessary background for a proper understanding of Grey Owl's work.

No lover of wild life or of literature should miss reading Grey Owl's own books.   H. C.

ACKNOWLEDGMENT

THE author and the publishers acknowledge with thanks the courtesy of the National Parks Branch, Ottawa, in permitting the reproduction of the copyright material *Fall Activities of the Beaver,* written by Grey Owl, and also the photographs illustrating this volume.

The agents for Harper Cory's illustrated lectures on Grey Owl and the Beaver are The Lecture Agency, Ltd., Outer Temple, Strand, London, W.C.2

CONTENTS

ILLUSTRATIONS

GREY OWL AND THE BEAVER

A VISIT TO GREY OWL

IN olden days the fur-traders sang "*A-roving we will go*" as they paddled their canoes northward along a tributary of the great Saskatchewan River. They journeyed far and wide to meet Red Indians willing to barter pelts of beaver, fox, raccoon, bear, wolf and other wild animals. Now we are to follow the old fur-trails into the wilderness until we arrive at a log cabin set beside a shimmering lake. There, many miles distant from the great cities, we shall meet an Indian whose fame has spread throughout the civilized world. Red Indians call him *Wa-sha-quon-asin*, which means "He who travels by night " : we know him by the name of Grey Owl.

We are more fortunate than the fur-traders. They propelled their long canoes over thousands of miles of waterways, enduring heat and cold, rain and wind cheerfully. Often enough rapids checked their progress : at such times the paddlers would unload their stores upon the bank, carry the canoes and bundles along the shore until the rapids lay in the rear, re-load their vessels and recommence paddling with a will, singing, perhaps, "*Send her on along, along : Send her on along,*" or, if it were near evening, they might chant the well-known refrain :

"*Row, brothers, row, the stream runs fast,*
The rapids are near and the daylight past."

The first part of our journey is made by motor car, and as we rush northward along the highway from the city of Prince Albert, we can visualize the trappers of a century ago toiling along this route : but, in those days there was no road. There was only a trail beaten hard by moccasined feet. Our car is dwarfed by the splendid pine trees as the road crosses the Nisbet Forest Reserve ; martens and squirrels playing in the tree-tops scamper from branch to branch along their tree-highways so swiftly as we approach that we obtain only fleeting glimpses here and there of bushy tails.

Emerging from the pine belt, our road leads for fifteen miles through a district of very large farms. We then leave the farmhouses in the rear and enter rolling country heavily timbered with unusually tall and beautiful poplars. The scene is one of wildness so entrancing that we are still admiring the view when we arrive at the boundary of Prince Albert National Park.

A park in the wilderness ? Yes, a park ; but the term is rather misleading, because Prince Albert Park is almost equal in size to one-quarter of the whole of Wales. It is a lovely region densely covered with birch, spruce, pine and poplar trees ; and although there are no patterned beds of choice flowers, such as delight the eyes in city parks, there are innumerable patches of various hues to mark the presence of wild flowers.

We are reminded at the boundary that heavy

penalties await any person who may be found with an unsealed firearm inside the park. For this region is a sanctuary where giant moose, comical black bears, dainty deer and industrious beaver are allowed to live without any human interference. A great variety of birds is found here, and some of them, especially the pelican and the cormorant, can be very humorous at times.

The pelican, with large mournful eyes and huge gullet pouch, always reminds me of a dignified churchwarden who has found a button on the collection plate and does not know whether to smile or to be angry. The bird looks clumsy as it waddles along the ground, but it has much grace when in flight. One would expect these ponderous creatures to be awkward on the wing ; instead, they make a splashy start until they get into the air, then they rise easily and rapidly, sometimes ascending so high that they vanish from sight.

The double-crested cormorant is quite a dandy during the mating season. Not content with a black plumage bronzed to greenish shades, he needs must grow a tiny tuft of feathers over each ear : thus he earns the name of "double-crested." Unlike most dandies, he is a hard worker who has reduced food-gathering to a fine art. The cormorants form a line across the mouth of a shallow bay, then paddle shoreward driving the fish before them. As the enclosed area becomes smaller and the fish are packed together, the birds dive below the surface, catch fish, toss them aloft, catch and swallow them as fast as they can. At last the fish, unable to travel forward any farther, turn and rush outward past their enemies. The birds dive and toss fish furiously for a minute or two. Then the cormorants move to another spot and recommence their fishing operations.

An officious Canada blue jay greets us with a derisive whistling as we enter the park. We ignore him and drive him to the summit of a small hill from which we feast our eyes on a pageantry of graceful trees, green meadows and prairie flowers. This, our first peep at the park, makes us anxious to be on our way. But now our speed is reduced so that we may not miss too many of the glories of the streams and lakes fringed with giant timber. We pause at Big Bluebell Tower, a forestry watch-tower rising from a grove thickly carpeted with bluebells.

Our road rises gradually from this point until, topping a low ridge, we see Waskesiu Lake stretching before us for nearly twelve miles. In the centre of the green-hued lake is pine-crowned King's Island posed like a sailing vessel at anchor. A short run downhill brings us to Big Beach with its clear white sands. The old fur-traders would have required days to travel the distance which we have covered in a matter of hours in a motor car.

We can travel no farther in the car, because we must follow the water trail down Waskesiu Lake. While the driver finds a guide for us, we cook and eat lunch, imagining ourselves to be as adventurous as the backwoodsmen of old. The meal ended, we help the guide to stow our stores in the canoe, then leaving the car among some poplars near the beach, we clamber aboard for our thirty-mile trip to Kingsmere.

Our guide, who is half Indian and half English, uses no compass, and we marvel at the skill with which he shapes our course. Pitying our ignorance, he points out landmarks which he uses as signposts. Green-clad Prospect Point is his first bearing, then westward to where a belt of magnificent white spruces mark

18

Clare Point. Now we cross a wide bay, keeping King's Island on our right. Due west of the island, two long green peninsulas jut outward, and cradled between them is a sheet of water which our guide calls Twin Point Bay.

We pass many capes and inviting bays, our guide having a name for each of them. The north shore begins to close in until but a mile of water separates the two shores. Three miles higher up the lake the two shores are pinched together, leaving only a narrow strait between them. Here we surprise Mother Duck and her family, who look like small balls of fluff as they paddle to safety in a straight line. The First Narrows, as the strait is called, is short, and soon we enter a wider section of the lake.

As we float through a strait called the Second Narrows, we see a giant moose eating water-lily pads. She snuffles and noisily blows water from her nostrils, paying little or no attention to us. We know that the creature is a cow moose because she has no antlers : only the bulls carry horns. Now we enter the most beautiful section of Waskesiu Lake, where capes overlap each other and shelter quiet, picturesque bays fringed with tree trunks almost to the water's edge. We cross to the north shore of the lake, and sail up the mouth of a silent stream which glories in the name of Kingsmere River. Our route, for the first two miles, lies through a thick forest of white birch, poplar, spruce and willow. The flow of the water is so light and gentle that paddling is easy. Evidently this district is a favourite with the creatures of the wild, for wild ducks are numerous, and here and there we see the russet red summer coats of deer who have been drinking until our approach alarmed them.

Our guide steers shoreward, and all hands work to unload the canoe : there are rapids ahead. The fur-traders who used this route had to carry every package : we use a wagon and push it along the light railway until we have passed the rapids. Within a few minutes we are afloat once more, and hurrying along the last three-quarter-mile stretch of the river. Suddenly we notice that the colour of the water has become green—we have reached Kingsmere Lake. A few minutes later we see a log cabin on the edge of the shore. The door is opened, and a man steps out into the sunlight. Our journey is ended, for Grey Owl stands before us.

Beside Kingsmere Lake

Tall, dressed in a suit of buckskin heavily fringed with leather laces, and with his long glossy hair braided, this striking person might have been conjured out of the pages of Fenimore Cooper's *The Deerslayer*. His friendly smile and cheery greeting reminds us that he is the Beaver Man, not the Deerslayer. We are not invited to enter the hut : having seen our cameras, Grey Owl encourages us to secure good photographs while the light is strong.

He whistles, and a squirrel appears almost miraculously on a branch overhead, but, being a perverse little creature, he bobs about here and there, never staying in one spot long enough to enable us to take a satisfactory picture of him. Adding insult to injury, he cries " Gurr-r-r-r ! " frequently, as though saying, " Who said *you* could photograph wild life ? "

Grey Owl now leads us to a quiet spot on the lakeside and motions to us to sit quietly and to watch. Placing his hands before his mouth, he calls his beaver people shoreward. Minutes pass slowly, and we wonder if the animals are sleeping soundly in their lodges. Then, when least expected, three beaver paddle swiftly in-shore to greet their friend. He stoops and talks quietly to them before he stretches out his arm to stroke their heads. They make a noise which is very much like the yapping of happy puppies, dive head first under the surface, and swim away.

Grey Owl looks at us inquiringly. Realizing that we had been so enthralled watching him and his beaver that we had forgotten to take any photographs, he smiles and good-naturedly calls other members of his family : this time our cameras click merrily when two beaver come to accept the petting of the naturalist. Back to the cabin we hasten, and, while we maintain silence, Grey Owl attracts Whiskey Jack, a wild blue jay which eats food from his hand. We had been unable to photograph the squirrel : without any difficulty, this friend of the wild creatures persuades Mr. Fluffytail to climb to his shoulder while we take snapshots of the man and the animal.

When the shadows begin to cloak the woods, we follow Grey Owl into his wilderness home. It is a very simple abode consisting of one large room, one side of which is fenced for the use of the two beaver, Jellyroll and Rawhide. They have taken possession of their share of the room, and have piled much mud and many sticks against the wall. There is another pile of sticks and mud against the outer wall, and thus the cabin logs form a division across a beaver lodge. The two beaver allow Grey Owl to use the remainder of the room as his living and sleeping quarters.

The room is quietly furnished with a stove, table, chairs, cupboards and a wide bunk : the walls are decorated with Indian designs painted on parchment, and also a few pictures of Grey Owl's wife, Pony, and of the beaver. The naturalist smiles when we ask him if he ever feels lonely in this cabin so distant from the nearest settlement. He places his hand upon a knob, and at once the cabin is filled with the strains of a dance band playing in Winnipeg almost six hundred miles away to the east.

Suddenly the door is shoved open, and in comes a large beaver, her arms laden with twigs. She waddles on her hind legs across the floor in a most solemn fashion, places her load upon the pile, and gives a grunt of satisfaction. She pays no attention to us, but, walking over to Grey Owl, clutches the leg of his trousers with a forepaw, and scolds as she tugs the deerskin.

" This is Jellyroll," says our host by way of introducing the animal. She must weigh at least sixty pounds : her incisor teeth look so strong and powerful that we lift our legs out of her reach. She might be friendly—but she might want to nibble our legs : it is better to be sure than to be sorry. Grey Owl gives her an apple which she eats with great enjoyment ; after which, sitting upon her large flat tail, she combs her silky fur, using the split nail on the second toe of each hind foot as a comb. When that task has been done to her satisfaction, the naturalist stoops to pet her, talking quietly to the animal, which replies in dreamy, contented tones. Then, wonder of wonders, Jellyroll places her head on the man's knees and falls asleep.

In walks a second beaver. This sedate, dignified creature is Rawhide, the male, who goes to Grey Owl and talks quietly. He is asking for an apple in beaver language. Upon receiving it, he goes outside, taking not the slightest notice of us strangers. Aroused by our conversation, Jellyroll crosses the room to inspect each of us in turn, grunts, as if saying, " Hm ! Of no importance," and goes outside.

As befits their importance as film stars—for Jellyroll and Rawhide are the chief actors in four films which have been displayed in almost every country in the world—the two beaver can enter or leave the log cabin at any hour of the day or night. Grey Owl imposes no restrictions upon them, patiently allowing them to use his property as though it belonged to them, and never rebuking them, even when they gnaw through the legs of chairs or table.

2

GREY OWL'S FRIENDS

GREY OWL has an enormous wealth of stories about his animal friends to recount, and one cannot listen to him for long without realizing that he is a genuine naturalist, not a scientific analyst posing as a naturalist. Our library shelves are overloaded with volumes describing the appearance and chief habits of wild creatures : many of them reach my study for review every year, but receive little welcome. The compilers of such books pride themselves upon their unsentimental attitude, and are scrupulously careful to record generalizations affecting the majority of the members of a species. This method may be of service to certain branches of science, but it is not natural history at its best, for the simple reason that no two animals of a given species are ever exactly alike, nor will they react to the same stimuli in precisely the same manner at a given moment. Animals, like human beings, are individuals with personal experiences, impulses and reactions. Under these circumstances, the items of out-standing interest and value are the intimate details of an animal's existence which the scientific catalogue-compiler overlooks.

A friend of mine obtained a baby grey squirrel, placed it inside a cage, and zealously recorded its appearance and habits. Terrified by captivity and the hourly scrutiny by the biologist, the animal died within ten days. I obtained a squirrel only ten days old, gave him the freedom of my study, won his friendship and studied him unobtrusively. The animal lived in my study for ten months, making no effort to escape, even though the doors and windows were left open, and I was able to collect a mass of information not to be found in natural history books about squirrels. Thus I learned that the grey squirrel can be very affectionate towards one person, that he has a lively sense of private property values, that he will fight bitterly to protect his own territory, that he will eat vegetable or animal food, and that he has fifty major and many minor sounds which form a language understood by other mature squirrels of the same species. At another time I was friendly with a skunk who visited my Manitoban bungalow daily for scraps, kept my place free from mice and behaved in a most gentlemanly fashion to me, although he almost slew my neighbour with his filthy scent-gun.

The cold, scientific attitude of the orthodox observer does not encourage the animal to relax and to act naturally. A cat stalking sparrows in the garden crouches and stares fixedly at his prey, and apparently some unique sense warns the hunted that it is in danger, so that it decamps or increases its vigilance. Man is but an animal, and the intensive observer is much like the cat stalking sparrows : his very concentration conveys a warning to the creature under observation, which immediately checks its free activity and becomes cautious and super-vigilant. When, on the other hand, wild creatures realize that a certain human being has sympathy with them, and that there is no need for them to maintain a nerve-straining vigilance in his presence, they eagerly respond to his advances by relaxing and betraying individual characteristics which may not be generally associated with wild animals.

Unfortunately the wild animal, once its confidence has been won, becomes so tame and trusting that it makes no allowance for the different attitude of strangers, and it may pay the penalty in pain and shock or even death. Horace, a red squirrel, visited me daily at Ninette, Manitoba, and loved to play with a string which I would dangle for him. One morning I was handling a live wire, and forgot that Horace was in the room. He gripped the wire and received a shock which almost made him stand on the tip of his tail with surprise : he darted from the room and it was ten days before I saw him again.

Grey Owl's method of winning the entire confidence of his animal friends is the only channel by which one can fully explore the daily activities and mental processes of these individuals which are in many ways so human. He has succeeded to such an extent that most of his animal friends lower every barrier of restraint, and he must ever be vigilant in his efforts to avoid causing them pain or shock.

The conduct of his beaver offers a good

example. Beaver are extremely alert creatures which mistrust every strange scent and sound until they have explored it carefully, and they take elaborate precautions to ensure their own safety when engaged in tree-felling. Yet Grey Owl's beaver have such implicit faith in the ability of their human friend that they calmly sit on the bank while he cuts down a tree which will crash to earth but a few feet away from them. One faulty stroke of the axe might cause the timber to drop upon the animals, but apparently they cannot imagine him making such an error. Needless to say, he has not tried an experiment to see how they would behave did a tree fall towards them : on the contrary he prefers to fell timber as far away from them as possible.

A muskrat gave her confidence to Grey Owl so completely that, of her own free will, she installed her family under the floor of a corner of the cabin. During the summer she would enter the cabin by the door, scratching and snuffling, if it was closed, until Grey Owl opened it for her : in winter she used a tunnel. This unnatural mode of living, due to Grey Owl's encouragement, led to an accident by which the animal broke a hind-leg. She continued to visit the naturalist, though less frequently. Fortunately the injured limb healed completely, enabling the rat again to come every day.

Squirrels can be extremely affectionate and trusting, in which case they tend to be " one-man " creatures, and extremely pugnacious to strangers. One small, lonely looking red squirrel more or less adopted Grey Owl, answering his call eagerly by travelling from bough to bough at lightning speed, and launching himself from a suitable limb on to Grey Owl's head, shoulders, or whatever part of his body was convenient. Like most tame squirrels, he would run under and about the man's feet as he walked : sometimes he would dart ahead a few yards, pause, look at Grey Owl and chatter as if saying, " Gosh ! You *are* slow for a six-foot crittur ! " At other times he would dart up Grey Owl's clothing and, head first, delve into various pockets in search of bread or other food, of which he was sure to discover a supply. Should he be out of sight on any occasion, a few loud calls would bring him along as fast as he could travel.

Like the beaver, he trusted Grey Owl without

reserve, and at times his activities when wood was being cut almost led to his extermination by the axe or the saw. At such times his curiosity and playfulness interfered considerably with the work in hand, and his perpetual motion compelled Grey Owl to watch where he placed his feet and his tools : in fact, Fluffytail was an adept at making a nuisance of himself. One day the squirrel entered the camp and began to investigate everything available : I know of no creature more inquisitive than the squirrel, unless it be Fisher, a member of the weasel group. Fluffytail found a mouse-trap—or perhaps the trap found him. The animal pulled himself free immediately, but not before he had received injuries which disciplined his spirits. He was greatly subdued and unsteady in his gait next day : then he suddenly disappeared. He had paid the penalty for being over-confident, despite Grey Owl's care.

One must have shared the friendship of a squirrel to be able to appreciate how greatly Grey Owl missed his jolly and charming visitor. Squirrels are the most fascinating companions imaginable, producing some new trick or characteristic daily. This individual had become

Grey Owl and the Whiskey Jack

a member of the family, and his absence made the yard seem empty and unusually vast. The snow covered his usual trails and haunts, and other but less interesting squirrels appeared upon the scene. Two of the new-comers were tamed and were learning to eat from Grey Owl's hand when, suddenly, the original Fluffytail returned in time to see what, to him, must have been an act of desecration. He had been absent for seventeen days : he proved instantly that he was in splendid condition and very ready to do battle for his rights and privileges.

Grey Owl was feeding one of the new-comers at one moment : the next instant there was a flash of red fur, a brief struggle, and the would-be usurper was in full flight leaving the spoils to Fluffytail. Readers may find it difficult to believe that Grey Owl could immediately recognize his squirrel, but that difficulty disappears when one remembers that members of a species vary physically and in their personal characteristics as freely as do human beings. It would be difficult, if not impossible, to find even two bees with exactly similar feet or habits. After a few days' close association with an animal, an intelligent person should be able to detect that creature though surrounded by a host of its kind. Grey Owl has expressed the opinion that the appearance of the head forms the chief means of identification. Certainly he has no trouble in distinguishing the muskrats and beaver at Kingsmere, although in the case of beaver he is assisted by the voice, actions, build and shape of the tail of each animal.

Despite all his care for the welfare of his animal friends, it sometimes happens that individuals will rely upon Grey Owl to the extent that he becomes the innocent cause of some slight harm to them. Such incidents are never repeated, but the naturalist must assume a form of guardianship over every animal which confides in him, and many must be the nights when care for his protégés keeps sleep from his own eyes.

Grey Owl would be among the first to admit that interference with Mother Nature is fraught with danger for wild life, for he has seen the results of such attempts at benevolence. Beaver, always very adaptable animals, made their home inside the camp, and it would be reasonable to expect, once they became accustomed to camp life, that they would be able to do everything

34

essential for their well-being. Such was not the
case. Mother Beaver, desirous of maintaining
contact with Grey Owl, whom she had known
all her life, wished to keep open a hole in the side
of the lodge leading into the cabin. The warmth
in the beaver-lodge was created by the bodies
of the seven occupants. The aperture in the
cabin would have allowed the warmth to escape,
while cold damp air from the water-filled tunnel
would have taken its place. The continual loss
of heat would have weakened the animals, and
they would have sickened rapidly because of the
mother's error. No wild beaver could have
made this miscalculation. Grey Owl adjusted
matters by plugging the hole, and Father
Beaver, who has had experience as a wild
creature, nobly assisted him from the inside of
the tunnel.

Two moose, one of them a four-year bull,
visit the camp frequently and make themselves
very much at home near the cabin. They inspect
the beaver works, and allow Grey Owl to
approach to within a few feet of them. The
bull will spend night after night near the camp,
quite undisturbed by human voices. He listens
attentively when spoken to, holding his head

in a manner which suggests that he understands what is being said. If he is decamping in alarm, a friendly voice will check his flight. Such conduct on his part is desirable, but it might lead to sudden death were he to wander beyond the sanctuary of the Park.

Moose are my favourite animals. They look fearsome and ungainly, but they are most intelligent and blessed with delightful traits. Deer graze, but moose browse : and even baby males will show the family chivalry by stretching their necks to secure the higher foliage while they leave the lower leaves and twigs for the females. An amusing feature of moose life is the day nursery to which the cows bring their offspring, leaving them all day in the care of two or three old cows for tuition in social conduct. Moose heads are considered valuable hunting trophies, but I have no admiration for the hunters. *Mouswah* (eater-of-wood), as the Sioux Indians call the moose, prefers to retreat silently before man if possible, unless cornered, wounded, or love-sick. A mating bull drove three of us into the branches of a tree and kept us there four hours. Stuffed heads of defunct bull-moose make me think that intelligent

animals were slain by less worthy creatures :
destruction, especially from a safe distance, is
not an occupation requiring intelligence.

Wild animals, however, speedily recognize a
sanctuary, and they will haunt such an area once
they have discovered it. Grey Owl considers
that they make this discovery by intuition. He
was not surprised, therefore, when a male deer,
probably attracted by the beaver works and by
a feeling of security from harm, began to show
a daily increasing interest in the camp. The buck
did not relax his vigilance and his mistrust of
man too readily, for he would manifest his pro-
found disapproval of any noise made by Grey
Owl. If, during his scavenging expeditions in
the yard, he were disturbed by the swinging of
the cabin door, he would erect his bushy white
tail and bob away like a released " Jack-in-the-
box." As though ashamed of his conduct, he
would suddenly halt after travelling a few yards,
and nibble the grass in an attitude of assumed
indifference, as though he had fled simply because he needed a little exercise.

The beaver at the camp have become so
accustomed to the presence of the deer that they
no longer plunge to a watery refuge when they

hear the noises of the two larger creatures. Unlike wild beaver, they continue with the work in hand, so causing an unnatural and dangerous state of affairs. There are many black bears in the Park. Although they are not encouraged to visit the camp, individuals prowl round the cabin at times, probably impelled by curiosity, but possibly because they desire beaver kitten for lunch. There is always the danger that the beaver might mistake the approach of Bruin for that of the moose, particularly if the breeze were blowing inshore. As a result, Grey Owl must make daily inspections of the nearby forest trails to prevent any disastrous visit of black bears to the beaver colony.

Every species of bird and animal appears to have a code of noises by which individuals can communicate one with another. Some species, however, appear to communicate soundlessly. I have on three occasions observed vixens recalling their cubs without uttering a sound which I could appreciate, and I have had ample proof in the field that Virginia deer can communicate in this manner. Evidently the Canada blue jay, better known by the Indian name of whiskey-jack (*wis-ked-jak*), possesses this puzzling gift, for two jays which took up their abode near Grey Owl's cabin invited all their friends to join them. According to Grey Owl, it would seem that all the whiskey-jacks tenanting a radius of five miles responded to the call, so many of them have come.

Inveterate cadgers and most accomplished thieves, the jays accompany Grey Owl when he goes on his daily tours of inspection. They are actuated, beyond any shadow of a doubt, by cupboard love, yet they have the grace, or are prompted by guilty consciences, to try to hide this, and to look very innocent and indifferent should Grey Owl but glance at them. At the same time they watch his every action like so many hawks watching a sparrow, and nothing eatable can escape their immediate attention. Trusting the naturalist, they will perch on his hand to peck at proffered food, or they may swoop and snatch the food in passing. But when one has said the most unkind things about whiskey-jacks—and I have had my hot breakfast stolen from the frying-pan by one— it must be admitted that they are cheery, jolly little creatures which make the forest ways more pleasant and sociable by their presence, and their song, simple and plaintive though it be, drives away depression from the mind of the lonely backwoodsman.

In his efforts to ameliorate the lot of many creatures, Grey Owl slightly upset the life of some squirrels. The Canadian red squirrel cannot be termed sociable, and, as far as my field observations show, all squirrels have a pronounced sense of territorial rights and a militaristic method of defending them. While the injured Fluffytail was absent undergoing treatment by Doctor Nature, Grey Owl gained the friendship of two other red squirrels. After the return of the healed patient, Grey Owl was accompanied to and fro among the timber by three tiny creatures filled with admiration for the naturalist, but with a most unholy desire to exterminate two hated rivals in the most painful manner devisable. In accordance with squirrel law each regarded the camp as his especial territory and deeply resented the intrusion of the others.

Grey Owl attempted to adjust matters by feeding each squirrel in a special district, but without success. For when food is plentiful and obtained with ease, frugal Fluffytail caches a portion of it and yells a warning to all creatures that his store must not be molested under penalty of sudden death. Naturally the other squirrels investigate at once, and what appears to be a battle-royal ensues. Actually it is a mild affair, for although the attack be venomously bitter, the attacked is a past-master in the science of retreat, but in the meantime the third squirrel may have taken an opportunity to raid the cache !

Members of various species of animals and birds have yielded to the sympathetic attention of Grey Owl, and where several species congregate in the same small area, it is inevitable that minor discords shall at times arise. Beaver have no excess of affection for the humble muskrat, and they seem to enjoy slapping the smaller creatures with their tails whenever they invade beaver territory. Four muskrats living under Grey Owl's cabin grew tired of being slapped when traversing the beaver works : they intelligently adjusted the situation by making a fresh tunnel to and from their underground hotel.

Muskrats can administer severe injuries with their teeth. Having seen how effectively they

41

can mangle human limbs, I, for one, would never attempt to pick one up except by the tail. Grey Owl, on the other hand, will thrust his arm down the muskrat tunnel and freely handle the animals. The creatures have such implicit faith in the man that they make no attempt to bite him—a fact which to my mind is extraordinary. One of these muskrats will sit up to beg for food, eats out of a dish or from the hand, and trots about the camp with all the assurance of a legal tenant. He will also answer Grey Owl's call, whether the call be for him or for some other creature.

Muskrats are extremely courageous, and they rarely hesitate to fight to preserve their liberty : this fact probably accounts for the belief among trappers that the animal is very vicious. Grey Owl is convinced that the muskrat will give proof of a more amiable disposition if treated with kindness. There is little room for doubt that he is correct on this point, for when an injured muskrat crawled across the floor, Grey Owl picked it up and probed gently in an attempt to locate the damage. When he touched the injured limb, the animal trembled, and gently nibbled at his fingers in its attempt

42

to advise him that he had touched the injury.
Even though it was the first time Grey Owl
had actually handled the creature, the muskrat
showed neither anger nor fear. This slight
incident commands my warmest admiration :
I do not know of a second man who would
have lifted an injured muskrat in this manner,
but I do know scores of experienced trappers
who would have shunned the task, and have
considered themselves amply justified.

The average visitor to the cabin by the shores
of Kingsmere Lake may possibly sympathize
with Grey Owl because of his lonely life. The
sympathy is wasted, for though the furred and
feathered company be absent when strangers
are present, they are not far away : Grey Owl is
never without a large and varied band of clients.
There are muskrats under a corner of the cabin
floor, beaver in their lodges, a skunk is probably
day-dreaming in an empty tent, squirrels are
poking inquisitive noses round the boles of
poplars or birches, a dainty deer or lordly moose
is hidden by the foliage ; in the trees the
whiskey-jack mimics the whistle of a visitor,
while from the lake comes the mournful call
of the loon or the trumpet honking of the

Canada wild-goose. The company is extensive, if hidden.

And at night the silence of the forest is disturbed at intervals by slight noises, most of which would be undetected by the townsman. Few of them escape the ear of Grey Owl, and each sound conveys to him a picture as vivid as though he had witnessed the incidents with his eyes. Thus by day and by night he is made aware of the presence and the activities of the creatures which dwell under his protection in the sanctuary of Waskesiu—all of them his friends.

3

GREY OWL MAKES A START

GREY OWL is such a charming host that we would like to stay longer with him, but the mournful hooting of an owl warns us that the moon is flooding the water-trail with yellow light to guide us back to our distant car. We enter the canoe, Grey Owl pushes it from the shore and wishes us " Good-bye and good luck." He stands waving to us, a lonely figure on the shore, until a bend of the land hides him from our view.

Many men would find his life impossible because of its isolation, but it is the life he deliberately chose. His intense sympathies are so wide and varied, and he has so many furred and feathered intimate friends, that he has no time for loneliness. Waskesiu and its surroundings form a paradise to him. Kingsmere Lake, five miles wide and six miles long, lies in front of his cabin, its crystal clear waters having a depth of one hundred and fifty feet in places. Rich forests clothe its shores, and here and there may be found groves of white birch, the most beautiful of all Canadian trees. The region is a place of beauty and inspiration. Here it was that Grey Owl conceived *The Pilgrims of the Wild,* one of the most charming and fascinating animal books in the English language, full of word-pictures of the wilderness and its creatures : the beauty and charm of the book are reflections of the beauty and charm of Kingsmere Lake.

Born in 1888, Grey Owl is the son of a full-blood Apache Indian woman and of a Scotsman who served as a scout under the renowned Buffalo Bill at Fort Laramie, Wyoming, U.S.A. Hating the cruelties and the injustice of the wars against the Red Indians of the prairies, the Scotsman resigned from his post as a Government servant. Grey Owl, however, had come in contact with Buffalo Bill, and when the latter visited Europe with his Wild West show, the youth came with them. The call of the wild appealed strongly to this young man who was skilled as a hunter and trapper, and, upon

his return to America, he made his way northward into Canada.

Men eager to dig untold wealth out of the
earth rushed to Cobalt, Ontario, when silver
was discovered there in 1905. Guides and
packers were greatly needed, and Grey Owl
found many demands for his services, guiding
miners and surveyors over forest trails, carrying
stores in his canoe, and packing heavy loads
across rough country. Packing is work for
strong men, not weaklings. Perhaps a load of
stores weighing over one thousand pounds is
to be packed inland, the journey being through
thick forest and over rock-strewn trails. The
packer divides his load into parcels of about one
hundred and fifty pounds each. He perches
the first parcel upon his broad shoulders, and
carries it along the trail until he requires a rest.
The load is then placed on the ground, but,
instead of sitting or lying down, the packer
returns for a second parcel; he rests his shoulders
on the return journey. Thus he continues until
all the stores are at the first halt, then on he goes
to a second halt.

During these arduous days Grey Owl met
members of the Ojibway tribe of Indians, and

they appreciated him so highly that they adopted him as a member of the tribe, telling him many secrets of the wild. Living as they did, wandering from place to place, he fell under the spell of the northern forests, learning to love Ontario and to regard it as his own land. Spruce and poplar held attraction for him, and he roamed through the forests at the hour when dancing fireflies traced their shining network against a background of shadowy bushes and boughs. Therefore red men gave him the name "*He who travels by night*," as does the nocturnal grey owl.

Time flies fast in the wilderness because there are so many wonders to behold ; each foot of earth has a peculiar quota of things fresh and novel. Even the boughs and tree-tops present an ever-changing picture, and never two animals or birds are exactly alike. Thus the mysteries of the forest captured the loyalty and attention of Grey Owl as he guided parties of miners who recognized beauty only in lumps of heavy ore. While others stayed in snug dwellings during the winter months, he roamed through silent aisles of the forest in search of animals with luxurious furs. The woodland trails became as

Grey Owl in Indian dress

an open book to him, and he was offered employment as a forest ranger.

To and fro among the trees and heavy undergrowth he ranged for several summers, hunting with eye and nose for signs of fire which, unless checked immediately, would sweep noisily across the face of the wilderness, converting a verdant paradise into a graveyard wherein charred and blackened tree-stumps would act as memorials of many creatures roasted alive by the greedy flames. For young birds and old, rabbits, moles, badgers, squirrels and many other furry creatures become panic-stricken when smoke irritates their senses, and then, doubling and re-doubling as they seek safety, they become entrapped by the fire and perish.

When, in 1914, the smouldering embers of hatred and strife were fanned into flames in Europe, Grey Owl enlisted in the 13th Montreal Battalion, and later served overseas with them. He was twice wounded during his three years of active service, and, rendered unfit for further active service, he returned to his old life. His woodsmanship earned for him the appointment of Assistant Chief Ranger in a large forest reserve. His work necessitated long journeys, and in the course of a few years he became conversant with every part of the district : he knew the woodlands as well as the townsman knows the street in which he lives. The work became monotonous and tiresome : Grey Owl wanted to explore new territory.

His few possessions were packed and stored in a canoe, and Grey Owl paddled forth in search of new regions where he might hunt, trap, and, if necessary, act as a guide and canoe-man. He travelled more than two thousand miles by canoe during the seasons of 1926 and 1927. Although he journeyed by wilderness ways miles distant from the nearest road or railway track, he saw no beaver. Yet here and there were broken dams and white decaying lodges, mute evidence that beaver once had lived and prospered abundantly in these districts. Rabbits and foxes possessed the land, but caribou with unusually large cloven hoofs and unattractive antlers had been as little able as the almost human beaver to match the savage subtlety of the greedy, human wielder of traps, rifles and even poison bait. The caribou and beaver had been slain in vast numbers, and those which had survived the massacre had fled far and wide. Between the opening of the trapping season of 1925 and the close of the 1927–28 season, no less than 287,409 beaver pelts were placed on the market. More than a quarter of a million members of the same species had been slain within three years.

Sick at heart and disturbed at the disappearance of an animal respected by Red Indians, Grey Owl determined to create a sanctuary for beaver. He returned from the northern forests, and, after his marriage to Anahareo, descendant of a line of Iroquois chiefs, set his feet on the trail of sacrifice and hardship which was to lead to a sanctuary for beaver and world fame for Grey Owl and his courageous wife, Anahareo, or Pony. To appreciate what this naturalist has accomplished, we must glance at the story of the fur trade.

4

IN THE BEGINNING

MANY years before the White Man saw the shores of North America, Red Indians were lords over a vast domain. The immense open spaces and an abundance of simple food made them contemplative and philosophical, enabling them to see the work of the Great Spirit in everything around them. Animals, trees, birds, rocks, running water, clouds and storms were to them in some way connected with the "Master of Life": but the Indian did not probe very deeply into the matter. He was content with the thought that animals and other things had spirits, and he hoped that they would be friendly disposed towards him.

This attitude was quite impersonal, however. An Indian might kill a beaver, but its spirit would suffer no harm, he thought, if he returned its bones and any refuse to the water which was its particular element. At the same time, he would not kill a beaver for the mere sake of killing : he conserved the animals because he knew that he would require flesh to eat and furs for warmth at some future time. He studied the lives and habits of wild creatures that he might be a successful hunter when food was required in the wigwams of his tribe. Thus he discovered that beaver have many traits similar to those possessed by human beings; he called them " little Indians," and he noticed that beaver had uses other than that of providing fur and flesh for man.

Few were the forest trails in those days, because the undergrowth was rank and dense : it was easier and quicker to travel by canoe on lake and stream. Water finds its own level, and many of the streams would have dried up but for the work of countless beaver. These Royal Engineers of the animal world built their many dams which checked the flow of the water and kept the canoe trails open.

The value of the animals' work did not end there, however. When the warm breath of spring melted the snow and ice, a thousand and one streams hurried musically over rock and crag as they journeyed seaward. Groups of them united *en route* to form wide and deep rivers which plucked giant trees from the banks and on the surface tossed and twirled them like so many corks.

Many a thundering river had its dignity debased and its power humiliated when it hurled its foaming waters against beaver dams. The wooden barriers held, and the piling waters overflowed their banks to swirl round roots and trunks until they were forced across the high land to depressed areas ; there they spread across the low lands and formed new lakes, each of which formed a new canoe route. Countless Canadian lakes owe their origin to the work of bygone beaver. And the rich silt spread upon the beds of many lakes so formed but now dried up gave fertility to arid lands.

The Indians valued the beaver as a maker of canoe trails, and respected him for his perseverance and personal courage alike. The sagacious animal was a worthy model for any student backwoodsman, therefore the Indian advised his son to sing a hymn of praise to

Gitche Manitou, the Great Spirit, and to study Ahmeek, the beaver. This was a training which could not be surpassed.

Patient and clever was the Indian child who learned to approach near enough to the beaver to observe them at work. For while the animals laboured, one or more beaver maintained sentry-go, interpreting every noise of the wilderness with uncanny accuracy. The faintest strange sound, shadow or smell was sufficient to send them headlong into the water, splashing a warning to their fellows which was never disregarded. This trait taught the child to approach animals silently, and with the breeze blowing in his face.

When it was necessary for them to work on land, the beaver invariably made smooth paths down which they could hurriedly escape to the water if alarmed. They chose with great caution the trees which were to be felled, and took steps to avoid falling timber before the trees fell ; and the child learned from such behaviour to be cautious and prepared for every emergency. These and many other lessons did the Indian youth gain from the " little Indians," and he respected the animals accordingly. Out-standing among his fellows was the man who gained the tribal name of " Beaver."

Sometimes an Indian obtained a beaver kitten and carried it to his wigwam, there to be nursed and petted by the women and girls. And many an Indian squaw who had lost her child found consolation in nursing a beaver kitten. There were, therefore, many reasons why the redskin cared for and protected the beaver.

The Indians of the interior were in contact with another creature which provided them with many of the necessities of life. To these people, the bison was all-important, and they considered that the Great Spirit had given this animal to the red man as a mark of special favour. Bison meat is savoury, and the strong hide was used for making tough, durable tent-covers, clothing, and shields : bison hide bound a wooden shell into a rigid saddle, and hide-coracles were used as boats. The shaggy fore-locks of the bison were twisted and braided to form lariats and ropes : bison sinews were shredded, rolled on the hand and used as threads : the great thigh-bones were used in the making of traps, while squaws made combs, knives and spoons out of the bison horns. Nothing was wasted, and even bison-gall was used in medicine.

The Plains Indians did not practise agriculture, but made themselves dependent upon the enormous bison herds which, we are credibly informed, frequently contained as many as one million animals. The result was that Indian tribes wandered to and fro in the wake of the herds.

Other creatures fled pell-mell while the bison were migrating. First would come the advance guard of bulls scattered over miles of prairie, trampling eggs and nests and flushing wild birds before them. Prairie wolves and rabbits instinctively and speedily departed elsewhere as soon as the pungent scent of bison bodies assailed their nostrils.

Behind the slowly moving scouts would come column after column of bison in groups varying in size, each animal grazing as it travelled forward : with the cows would come the calves, carrying their heads low as they plucked the coarse grasses with their tongues. Ere long the prairie would assume a new appearance. Hummocks and mounds swept bare of vegetation would arise where but a short while earlier had been a flat sea of long buffalo-grass.

In early days, the Indians made elaborate preparations for the bison hunt. When the scouts reported that a herd had been sighted, the chief divided the tribe into four bands. Three bands of young men moved across the prairie in single file, marching throughout the afternoon and night. They would reach their hunting positions at dawn, forming three sides of a square round the herd, each hunter being posted at a considerable distance from his fellows.

Obeying a signal from the chief, the braves would set the dry buffalo-grass alight : as the flames leaped skyward, old men and women from the camp hastened to form the fourth side of the square. Panic-stricken by the smoke and flames the animals would bunch solidly together, enabling the Indians to slay cows and bulls and to secure hides and flesh sufficient for several weeks' consumption.

When the horse was introduced to the prairies, the Indians hunted in small parties and were content to kill fewer animals at a time. Then the hunt was a very different affair : the hunters literally carried their lives in their hands. The Indians would approach the bison about dawn, make a swift attack upon one flank of the herd, and immediately retire to safety. Bulls in the van of the herd would throw up their heads and bellow as soon as they saw or smelled the human beings. Then away they would wheel and escape at a plunging gallop, the herd immediately following in their trail. Column after column would thunder along, a mass of creatures rendered insane by sudden fear, covering the prairie like a dense, black, living sea. Yet even in their panic, the bison instinctively protected the calves, hustling them into the centre of the herd while the bulls took up position on the outer fringes. When the flying herd had disappeared and the curtain of dust raised by their feet had subsided, the Indians sought the carcasses of the bison pierced by their arrows. Sometimes, however, the Indians were trapped between columns of racing bison, and then the braves had cause to sing their death-songs. For although the male bison weighs much more than a ton and has an awkward method of running, he travels so swiftly that it takes an exceptionally good

59

cow-pony to keep up with him. There is little chance of escaping in front of him; in such cases the hunter tried to slay two or three of the leading bison so that their carcasses would become an obstacle splitting the herd, and providing a shelter for man and pony.

Beaver, bison, bear, wapiti, and many other creatures played their part in providing the red-skin with food and clothing. Because he realized that all things had been made by the Great Spirit and therefore had rights and privileges as concrete as his own, the Indian hunted only when necessity compelled. He had no thought of trapping that he might amass stores of luxurious furs by which his wealth of personal property could be advertised. To the contrary he regarded any amassing of personal property as an offence against mankind, for had not *Gitche Manitou* provided all things for the use of all men and their lower brethren?

The Indian shared in the work of collecting the tribal stores, and thanked the Good Spirit who supplied the hunting grounds to keep him alive. Before he smoked his pipe, he pointed the stem skywards, and this simple motion meant the prayer, " Great Spirit, give me plenty of meat : let me live in peace and comfort with my people, and remain long with my children." As the squaw lifted the meat-kettle from the fire, she would softly murmur, " Spirit, partake ! " : and each brave as he took his portion uttered a similar prayer, or, perhaps, threw a choice morsel into the fire that it might be consumed by the Great Spirit. In many ways the Indian associated animals with " the Father of all things " : therefore he conserved the wild creatures. And, perhaps the finest of his traits, he preferred to hunger rather than to kill female animals during the breeding season. But all this was before the White Man came to upset tribal customs and values.

5

DESTROYING ALL

ONE day, says a Red Indian legend, the Great Spirit saw three ships driven by fierce Atlantic winds beating toward the shores of Canada. He knew that the white strangers in the vessels would despoil the red men and their friends the Beaver People, the Fox People, the Deer People, and all the other kindly peoples of the wilderness. Bowed with grief, he entered the woods and departed from the sight of men for ever. The White Man landed, and the Forest People fled before him.

This legend is heavy with history. When the French settled on the banks of the St. Lawrence River, they were interested in beaver pelts more than in anything else : their settlements were principally fur-trading posts inhabited by fur-traders, and those who wished to till the soil received little encouragement. Beaver furs, highly prized in France, were sought eagerly, and men who knew little about trapping went into the woods to slay every beaver they might surprise. Red men brought beaver, fox and bear skins to the posts, bartering them for mirrors, blankets, knives and trinkets. Beaver! more beaver! was the cry, but the Indian was loath to hunt this animal too closely because tribal tradition demanded respect for it.

Liquor was offered for beaver skins, and tradition was washed away in a stream of " fire-water." Indians driven half-insane by a desire for liquor sought the beaver as feverishly as did the white trappers. Thousands of pelts were bartered at the trading-posts and shipped to France ; and the surviving beaver fled farther afield from the steady attack of the trappers. Explorers sought new beaver territories and, according to historians, trod the path of glory : it was a gory path carpeted with beaver pelts.

Northward went Radisson and Groseilliers seeking beaver, and finally they reached the shores of Hudson Bay. La Vérendrye and his sons sought beaver so far westwards that they gazed upon shining peaks which may have been the Rocky Mountains ; and La Salle followed the beaver-trail southward until he reached the shores of the Gulf of Mexico. Trappers hastened along the new trails, and trading-posts were built in the wilds : beaver, the trail-maker, was slowly opening the continent to settlement. Canoes heavily laden with pelts returned to Quebec, Three Rivers and Ville Marie (Montreal), and New France became prosperous and wealthy at the expense of the Beaver People. Beaver was the most important topic in the colony, and beaver skins were used as currency. Ships laden with 15,000 beaver skins sailed annually for France.

The success of the fur-traders was the weakness of New France. The English envied France her rich fur trade, and eagerly enlisted the services of Radisson and Groseilliers as guides to an expedition to Hudson Bay. The travellers returned to London with a rich cargo of beaver skins, and the Hudson's Bay Company was formed at once. Slowly the English established themselves round the shores of the Bay as powerful rivals to the French. Traders from the English colonies on the Atlantic coast invaded the French district of Louisiana to barter for the choicest furs under the very noses of the

Frenchmen. Strangely enough, the Spaniards of Texas and New Mexico sought only precious minerals, ignoring the beavers which inhabited creeks and streams in great numbers.

France and England went to war in Europe, and the echoes of the conflict resounded on the banks of the St. Lawrence. New France, which had devoted more attention to the gathering of beaver skins than to the creation of a population rooted to the soil, passed into the hands of the English : thanks to the selfish policy of the fur-traders, the colony was unable to defend itself once the garrison of Quebec had been outwitted, and the vast region of Louisiana was abandoned because defence was impossible.

The fur trade was now open to every man who cared to enter the woods ; settlers anxious to gain wealth easily followed the beaver-trails. Inexperienced as trappers, they slew the wild creatures humanely and inhumanely. Traps, poison bait and guns were used : animals suffered untold agonies before they died, yet nothing but fur was considered to be important. Fur-trading companies sent parties as far west as the Rocky Mountains to trade for beaver, and Indians who respected and would have conserved the animals

were tempted with spirits to trap the wild folk
and to lose their manhood. A flood of liquor
swamped the west, bringing destruction to the
beaver and degradation to the red man.

Fur companies fought ferociously among
themselves, each, with one exception, so anxious
to obtain beaver that they accepted every and
any pelt offered. The law of the woods observed by every experienced trapper is that the
female animal must be left undisturbed during
the breeding season. The avaricious traders
persuaded their hirelings to trap in and out of
season. Pelts taken during the breeding season
are poor in quality, but they were accepted by
all except the Hudson's Bay Company. Beaver
kittens were left parentless to perish, and adults
which survived the massacre sought refuge in
the depths of the northern forests. For many
years, half a million beaver pelts were exported
annually.

Internecine warfare reduced the fur companies to bankruptcy, and the Hudson's Bay
Company was the only large organization to
survive. Under the guidance of factors in
charge of the Company's trading-posts, liquor
was abolished from the beaver territories, and

the trapping of beaver during the breeding season was sternly discouraged. The Beaver People, given a respite, slowly returned to many of their old haunts.

The population spread and settled on the land, and the beaver, in company with other fur-bearers, retreated northward as towns and villages encroached upon the wilderness. Professional trappers and Indians who lived by hunting followed the animals, but there was no insensate slaughter, and the wild creatures were able to replenish their numbers during the breeding season. Improvements in the railroad and postal services paved the way for another mass attack on beaver, fox, muskrat and other animals. Fur-houses posted highly coloured literature to farmers and settlers, describing the riches to be gained by trapping, and also the so-called " best methods " of trapping animals. Amateurs bought traps and bait and hastened to the woods : few of them became rich, but the animals suffered because of the amateur's lack of trapping experience. The white man spoiled shamelessly where the Indian had conserved, and Canada was in danger of losing the animal regarded as one of her national emblems.

67

6

THE NATIONAL PARKS

A PARTY of travellers in Yellowstone Park
sat round a camp-fire at the close of a
summer day in 1879, and voiced their enjoyment
of the wild beauty around them. Cornelius
Hedges of Montana collated their views by
saying : "God made this region for all the
people and all the world to see and to enjoy
for ever. It is impossible that any individual
should think that he could own any of this
country for his own and in fee. This great
wilderness does not belong to us, but to
America. Let us make a public park of it,
and set it aside for America, never to be
changed, but kept sacred always just as it is
now, so that Americans always may know how
splendid this early America was, how beautiful,
how wonderful."

Men laboured with a will to give this vision

concrete form, and ere long the United States and Canada had set aside vast tracts of wild land to be maintained for ever as National Parks in which the wild animals and birds should find sanctuary. But although hunting regulations were made, they were not properly enforced. Roads and trails made through the parks for the benefit of visitors enabled hunters to approach their prey with greater ease, and the wild goat of the Rocky Mountains, in company with the Bighorn sheep, was sought and slain as big game : the two species were being steadily wiped out.

About the beginning of this century, men began to realize that natural conditions were being altered so violently that soon there would be few places where original conditions could be found. Several species of animals and many plants had been blotted out of existence, and many others were on the verge of extinction. Scientists who had devoted much time and thought to the study and classifying of the bones and families of animals and birds began to be interested in the *minds* of living animals. For a while they studied animals in zoos, but eventually they realized that the zoo animal, living an unnatural life, does not always reflect the conduct of the wild creature. However well he be provided for, no creature can act naturally unless he is living naturally. It has become increasingly difficult to study wild animals under natural conditions because of the decreasing number of wild creatures, and because of their increasing fear of man. These facts put forward by scientists showed the possibilities of National Parks as regions for the study of the minds and behaviour of wild creatures.

The bison had disappeared from the plains, and men mourned the departure of the " Monarch of the Prairies " until chance offered the Canadians a unique and romantic opportunity of possessing many bison. Walking Coyote, a Pond d'Oreille Indian, found two bull and two heifer bison calves in Southern Alberta during the summer of 1873. Obeying the Indian custom of caring for young and unprotected animals, he fed and tended the calves until he gave them into the keeping of the Mission of Saint Ignatius. The tiny herd prospered and rapidly increased, and ten bison were sold to Michael Pablo, a half-breed, in 1884.

Pablo grazed his herd on a portion of the Flathead Indian reservation in Montana, and their numbers increased enormously during the following twenty-two years. But when the United States Government opened the reservation to settlement in 1906, the half-breed did not know where to find food for the bison. The Government of Canada seized this opportunity to acquire a bison herd, and purchased 716 animals. Pablo was faced with a second problem; he had sold and had to deliver animals which had never been herded and which were as wild as their ancestors of olden days. Expert cowboys and the fastest ponies available were engaged, but rounding up bison is very much like taking pigs to market; the animals wanted to go each his own way, and three years passed before all the animals were loaded in trucks and delivered to the authorities in Alberta.

The bison had such great appetites that they ate themselves out of their first Canadian home. An area of nearly two hundred square miles was fenced off at Wainwright, as a wild-life sanctuary bearing the name of Buffalo National Park. The herd was transferred to Wainwright successfully, and before many years had passed it numbered 8,000 head. The park, however, could provide grazing for only 6,000 bison, and the herd had to be reduced. Some of the animals were shipped to a district near Fort Smith in the North-West Territories where a herd of scrub buffaloes roamed free. This sanctuary, known as the Wood Buffalo Reserve, covers an area about one and a half times the size of Wales ; it is the largest wild-life reserve in the world. Thousands of bison shipped thence from Wainwright have mingled amicably with the original inhabitants, and there is no longer any possibility that the bison will become extinct. The natural increase of the Wainwright herd since 1907 has exceeded 25,000.

Meanwhile it had been observed that another most interesting creature was rapidly disappearing—the pronghorn antelope. Many attempts made to secure and to protect it ended in complete failure, for this creature is one of the most difficult to provide for in captivity. Extremely sensitive, it resents any restriction of its freedom so keenly that it becomes delicate and short-lived. When treated as an exhibition animal, it looks jaded, spiritless, and almost lifeless ; it

Bison

requires a preserve so extensive that it does not realize that it is in confinement.

Pronghorns speedily respond to the friendly advances of human beings, and they will follow friends with dog-like affection and loyalty ; few animals can surpass them in affection and trust. The Royal Canadian Mounted Police guarded the few survivors in Southern Alberta and Saskatchewan, but as settlement proceeded apace and railroad and fences interfered with the normal roving habits of the animals, so shortening their lives, it was feared that the pronghorn would become extinct.

In 1908 Theodore Roosevelt called the attention of Americans and Canadians alike to the need for active conservation, because much that was priceless had already gone for ever from the control and the enjoyment of the people. It was pointed out that a National Park from which the original fauna had disappeared would be only an apology for a National Park. The two countries set to work with energy at once. Canada organized a National Parks Bureau under the control of Commissioner J. B. Harkin, a man of energy, imagination and determination, and the day of the extermination of animals in the parks ended abruptly. A system of patrols and inspections was established, a code of penalties for those who violated the sanctuary of the parks was drawn up, and Harkin saw that the laws were enforced and respected. The results surprised everybody.

Quickly realizing that they would find neither persecution nor violence of any kind within the parks, the animals lost all their timidity and mistrust of man ; they became noticeably tame. Within two years the wild animals began to return to the sanctuaries, and their numbers have been gradually restored. Various species which have used the parks as breeding grounds have spread beyond the park boundaries and have stocked the surrounding districts.

Bighorn sheep which had been taught by experience to shun man now allow visitors to approach within camera range. Gentle deer, ever on the alert, trespass on the gardens surrounding park headquarters to browse upon forbidden flowers, or to eat dainties from the hands of well-disposed strangers. Comical black bears visit camp sites to beg for food which is refused only with difficulty. Bruin is so persistent that notices requesting visitors not to feed bears or leave food about for them are posted in prominent places. This may seem to be unnecessary, but gifts to a bear bring an undesired response. Every species of animal has a series of noises which form the language of that particular unit of the animal world. For instance, the grey squirrel has fifty major and many minor noises, and apparently every grey squirrel understands them. Black bears have a small code of sounds, and though I have never discovered which is the sound for cake, it must be a well-known one, for if cake is given to a bear to-day, he will return at the head of many friends to-morrow, and the entire company will want cake.

The pleasure of being able to establish such close contact with delightful wild creatures, and to have the opportunity of studying or photo-graphing various species in their native haunts, is now one of the chief attractions of the parks ; it is also proving more satisfactory than hunting for an increasing number of people.

The National Parks Branch tried at first with little success to breed pronghorn antelopes in parks, but when the great opportunity came in 1914, the Commissioner acted rapidly and with genius. Word was received in Ottawa that a small herd of forty-two pronghorns had been seen feeding near Foremost, Alberta. The Branch knew to their sorrow that it was almost useless to take the antelopes to a park ; indeed, the sensitive creatures had a greater chance of surviving as they were. But if the animals could not be taken to a park, perhaps a park could be taken to the pronghorns !

While they grazed and gambolled to their hearts' content, workmen erected a fence round an area of 5,160 acres without alarming the antelopes ; twelve miles of fencing were used, and the captives had abundant space in which to roam without sensing captivity. The area became an antelope sanctuary bearing the name of Nemiskam National Park. It was a sheer gamble as to whether the experiment would succeed, and the Branch waited anxiously for results. But the gamble proved to be an out-standing achievement in wild-life conservation ; the herd has increased tenfold, and the pronghorn antelope has at last been rescued from the danger of extermination.

A publicity department under a very efficient director awoke Canadians to the fact that the parks were their property, and formed ideal places in which to spend a holiday and to see wild creatures at close quarters. The people were eager to explore their new recreation grounds, and nearly 55,000 visited the parks during 1914 ; the parks are now visited annually by over 600,000 people.

Although many people regarded the protected animals chiefly as curiosities, the more thoughtful visitors saw the value of conservation, and were disposed to treat all animals, wild and domesticated, with consideration. During the war period, however, when most of the experienced trappers deserted the forests and waterways in their eagerness to serve in fighting units as sharpshooters, trappers of a new type invaded the trails of the wilderness. They were inefficient and cared nothing about conservation, and worked destruction with much unnecessary cruelty.

The old trappers tried to trap animals in such a way that they were killed rapidly and with the minimum of pain ; and, desiring prime skins, they hunted during winter when furs, needed to keep their owners warm, were rich and thick. This method left the animals in peace during the breeding season, and they were enabled to produce young which balanced the number of creatures trapped during the previous winter. There is almost always a measure of cruelty and suffering connected with trapping, but the experienced trapper tries to be as merciful as possible, otherwise the anguished struggling of the trapped may cause damage to the fur.

The new-comers frequently used traps which were unsuitable for the type of animal sought, and creatures caught in weak traps dragged them away to their dens ; but hampered by the attachments on their legs, they were unable to seek food and died of slow starvation. Others badly caught bit off forelegs and limped away to freedom on three legs. Some caught in fiendish spring traps hung suspended in the air by one leg until they died from hunger and thirst and terror.

To supply the increasing demand for furs, the inefficient workers trapped adult animals during the breeding season, and wondered why they obtained low prices for the pelts so lacking in quality. Beaver and otters in particular suffered greatly, for with the destruction of the parents the kittens were left helpless. Beaver kittens rely upon the mother for food, and they require companionship: when the amateurs needlessly smashed open the lodges and made gaps in the dams, they cared nothing for the orphaned kittens wailing despondently for their parents. And the kittens which did not fall as prey to the hungry predatory animals crept inside their ruined homes, curled themselves on the bedding, and died slowly in loneliness.

Otters are amphibious, but the young do not take to the water instinctively: they are taught to swim by the mother. They eat fish, but the parents must teach them how to catch fish. Deprived of their parents, they cowered on the banks of streams, unable to escape predators by swimming to safety because they had not been taught, or starving to death while fish darted to and fro almost beneath their noses. The sounds of hungry, lonely and dying infants were added to the voices of the wilderness because in-efficient men wished to earn a few extra dollars. Animals had desirable pelts, but neither rights nor privileges. The creatures which survived the onslaught made new trails into the wilderness, and fled far from the trails of man. The old-time territories of beaver and other creatures became a desolation. The wapiti and the moose were more fortunate than their smaller brethren ; being chiefly forest creatures, they were more difficult to find, and they could seek safety with greater rapidity. Beaver disappeared over vast areas, and the end of the beaver-trail seemed to loom near at hand in several districts.

Settlements expanded, industrial and mining centres enjoyed a mushroom growth, aeroplanes droned northward carrying stores and personnel for new water-power developments, and immense areas of forest were reduced to ashes, sometimes purposely but more often through carelessness. The face of the wilderness was changed, and the Beaver People followed the Fox People into the land of the Caribou. Veteran trappers, wearied of seeking fruitful hunting grounds, talked about the fur-riches of other days, and shrugged their shoulders despondently as they accepted patronage and dollars from city-bred people desiring guides to lead them among the standing timber.

7

GREY OWL'S DREAM

GREY OWL came from his forest reserve into a forest region vastly changed during a few years, and he would have none of it. Launching his canoe, he began his journey along the beaver-trails into the wilderness. The widespread evidence of senseless destruction disgusted and made him heartsick : it was obvious to a woodsman as experienced as he that the beaver had not been given fair play. He returned to civilization convinced that the day of the trapper was drawing swiftly to its close : it seemed as if the National Parks would soon be the sole sanctuaries for beaver.

After their marriage, Grey Owl and Anahareo made their home in the forest. She had no love for trapping, and deplored the suffering it caused : necessity compelled her husband to seek and to obtain furs. As the days passed,

Grey Owl experienced a steadily growing distaste for the work. Then, when it was least expected, a simple incident occurred which made him abandon his beaver traps for ever.

When they were afloat in the canoe one day, Grey Owl and Anahareo saw two orphaned beaver kittens. Prompted by his wife, the trapper took the babies into camp and cared for them. Beaver kittens are extremely delicate little things and difficult to rear by hand, yet, much against all expectations, these babes of the woods thrived in a remarkable manner, becoming absolute monarchs commanding the services and attention of their human friends. Full of mischief and most affectionate, they thrust themselves upon Grey Owl in such a way that he was compelled to study them. They were privileged individuals, and persons require names. The Indians call the beaver *Ahmeek* : but as one name could not suffice for two creatures, one was called McGinty and the other McGinnis.

The task of rearing the two waifs made endless demands upon Grey Owl, but the affection and complete trust with which they repaid him bound him to the kittens as nothing else could

82

have done. He watched them at play and noticed the variety of ways in which they showed their intelligence. Solemn-looking animals, as are all beaver, they stared at him when he spoke to them, nodding their heads as though they understood, and sometimes uttering a puppy-like yapping as if in complete agreement. They could not understand his words, but they possibly knew from the inflexions of his voice whether he was pleased or displeased with their conduct. Grey Owl and Anahareo, for their part, learned to distinguish the inflexions of the beaver language until they knew when the animals were happy or sad, angry or uneasy, hungry or satisfied, and so forth. The noises of animals are strange languages to us until we have patience to study them.

The beaver, while still babies, showed that they considered that they had rights and privileges, and they were so determined to have their own way that Grey Owl decided to interfere with them as little as possible—to let them develop naturally. If, later, they should wish to live as do other beaver, he would not hinder them: therefore he gave them perfect freedom from the start. The kittens used the camp as though it belonged to them, considerately allowing Grey Owl and his wife to share a part of it. Mischief occupied much of their time, and the smiling naturalist tolerated their caperings. There was nothing else he could do, because the beaver were such jolly, friendly little people.

Their reliance and complete dependence upon him made Grey Owl consider the need for conservation. The beaver-trails had withdrawn from the haunts of civilization because adults had been slain, and thousands of kittens like McGinty and McGinnis had been left parentless to pine and starve to death. The mere thought of harming the kittens or of abandoning them to a lingering death was too painful to consider seriously. Yet, in the ordinary course of events, they might at a later date have been caught in traps to be battered to death for the sake of their furs, still affectionate and intelligent creatures desirous of trusting men were they but kindly.

The more he considered the matter, the more fiercely Grey Owl hated the idea of trapping beaver. Studying McGinty and McGinnis, he had, as it were, a vision of a large forest area studded with crystal streams and lakes in which many beaver worked and played and cared for their kittens, a place where guns were silent and traps unknown, a beaver sanctuary where men would visit the animals as friends rather than as destructive foes. It was a deeply moving idea, but the obstacles to be overcome were many and fearsome. Such an area would cost a fortune in money, and Grey Owl was not rich. The greatness of the man is shown by the fact that he determined to make his vision a reality, even though it seemed that he was attempting the impossible.

He resolved to abandon the trap-line and to consecrate his energies to the work of conservation. It was a tremendous resolution for any trapper to make, because he was turning his back upon his means of earning a livelihood. He had to seek new employment which would enable him to dwell in the woods where he might protect his beaver. He knew, and so did his wife, that great sacrifices would be necessary before his scheme could earn success : they counted the cost, and Anahareo encouraged him to become a conservationist.

McGinty and McGinnis were to be the first

tenants in the proposed sanctuary, but Grey
Owl wanted a larger population. There were
no beaver to be found locally, but rumour
said that many of them enjoyed life on the
shores of a Quebec lake. Grey Owl decided
to move to that locality. Camp was struck
and the little party journeyed southward, the
beaver travelling luxuriously in a box which
was sometimes carried on the shoulders of the
man. But when the naturalist reached Touladi
Lake, he discovered that beaver were extremely
scarce there : rumour had lied, and Grey Owl
had spent all his money on a fruitless journey.
Dismayed but undaunted, he pitched his camp
near the lake.

Having served as a soldier with the French-
Canadians of Montreal, Grey Owl found
himself among friends, and the kind-hearted
habitants of Touladi warmly welcomed the
new-comers, showing a sympathetic interest
in McGinty and McGinnis. Needing money
urgently, the naturalist began to write accounts
of the life of the wilderness as he knew it, and
sent them to magazines. His writings were
word-pictures of amazing beauty which made
the woods and forests appear before the eyes

of his readers, and his animal characters were virile living creatures. It was obvious that he was writing from experience, and his success as a writer began with his first article.

One of those early efforts gave me so much enjoyment that I hoped Grey Owl would write a book about beaver. I had read many books on the subject, but they lacked life and reality: in some cases they contained statements which I knew from personal observation of wild beaver to be foolishly inaccurate. Grey Owl's beaver were alive and convincing, and they behaved as did the animals I had seen at work and at play. He knew beaver intimately and sympathized with them, and he was a gifted writer : he was well qualified to write an outstanding beaver book.

The income derived by writing helped to support the tiny colony, but there were times when Grey Owl had difficulty in carrying on: still he persisted, refusing to admit defeat. One day McGinty and McGinnis went down to the lake : they never returned. Almost dazed by his loss, Grey Owl ranged the woods seeking his friends, but he had seen them for the last time. Their loss was a severe blow to him, because he had formed a deep, sincere regard for the two animals.

More determined than ever to establish a beaver sanctuary, he sought until he obtained a female kitten to which he gave the name of Jellyroll. At a later date he secured a male kitten which was christened Rawhide: and his hopes of founding a beaver refuge were renewed. The kittens made themselves very much at home at Touladi, but they could not take the place of McGinty and McGinnis in the affections of Grey Owl.

Grey Owl's articles attracted wide attention in the press, and editors asked for more. *Country Life*, in England, published some of his beaver stories, and *The Times,* drawing attention to his work, stated that he had " discovered an unsuspected talent for writing." A request for a book from his pen encouraged the naturalist to burn midnight oil. People visited the camp during the day to see the beaver, and when quietness descended upon the shack with evening dusk, *Wa-sha-quon-asin* laboured upon a graphic and eloquent description of a frontier rolling ever backward before the advance of civilization. McGinty and McGinnis appeared as the leading actors and humorists of the story, but trappers, miners, lumberjacks, Indians and others marched vividly across its pages. When the work was finished, it was typed by a French-Canadian who knew little English, and posted to England.

Those who visited Touladi Lake witnessed many unusual sights. Centuries of persecution have given wild beaver an instinctive mistrust of mankind, and the animals seek the nearest hiding-place when they detect his approach by sight, smell or sound. At Touladi, an intimate friendship existed between Grey Owl, Anahareo, Jellyroll and Rawhide. Indeed, the two animals behaved more like obedient house-dogs than children of the wild, and waddled awkwardly over the ground to answer their friend's call. Their behaviour was not based upon cupboard love : they were strong in the body, and abundant beaver food could be found near many a Quebec stream. There was nothing except affection to keep them at Touladi.

The beaver visited the camp whenever they took the fancy, but, as they grew older, they spent many summer hours among the rushes and water-lilies fringing the shores of the lake.

To seek them among the masses of weeds would be a task as thankless as that of seeking two needles in a haystack. When the naturalist wished to see his charges at such times, he would paddle his canoe to open water, smite the surface with the blade of a paddle to attract their attention, and send a call well known to them re-echoing among the many creeks. The wanderers responded immediately, swimming swiftly and gracefully to meet him like two tiny dark-brown submarines riding on the surface of the lake.

First one and then the other beaver clambered inboard when Grey Owl tilted the canoe and lowered a gunwale to make the ascent easier: they accepted petting before rising upon their hind legs to take the gifts which their friend never failed to produce. There was no ill-mannered snatching or vicious snapping for the slice of apple or potato. The food was taken daintily, after which the recipient slipped into the water, swam to the nearest floating sapling and dined. As became a perfect gentleman, Rawhide waited patiently in the background until the lady had been attended to.

This feeding of the beaver may seem to be a

very ordinary and unimportant trick : actually it requires great mutual trust on the part of both man and the animals, and courage on the part of the human being. Beaver, cutting across the grain, can take large shavings out of tree-trunks : if one of the animals felt dissatisfied and attacked Grey Owl, it could mangle his wrist with one bite. Fortunately both creatures are gentle and sweet-tempered, never molesting Grey Owl and Anahareo.

The principal food of beaver consists of the bark of poplar, willow, elm and birch, with juicy lily-pads as seasonal dainties. Jellyroll and Rawhide had gained a liking for cooked food as well, and they gave cause for laughter whenever Grey Owl placed a dish of boiled rice near the edge of the water. Table manners were ignored, and each little gourmet would clutch the food in a black hand, and stuff the rice into its mouth, hardly pausing to breathe until the meal ended. Apples and potatoes were welcomed with grunts of delight, whether bestowed or stolen : the beaver never hesitated to help themselves whenever they discovered eatables stored in hidden places.

If, however, one of the animals could not

find desired titbits, he or she would seek Grey Owl, and, standing erect beside him, would pluck at the leg of his trousers with a tiny hand. The attitude of the creature resembled that of a child begging for sweets, and its meaning could not be mistaken. Sometimes Anahareo would coax one of the beaver to wrestle with her, and although the animal weighed less than sixty pounds, the woman had to exercise all her strength to resist the attempts to push her backwards. There was no rough play on the part of the animal : on the contrary, it would gently rub its face against Anahareo's lips to bestow and to accept favours.

Wrestling, or a form of hugging and shoving which might well be called wrestling, is the favourite sport of beaver, and Jellyroll and Rawhide pitted their strength against each other on the land or afloat, grunting and straining until one tired of the tussle. The tired one would acknowledge defeat by submerging or by swimming swiftly away.

The beaver behaved naturally before visitors, and stories about them circulated far and wide. At the same time Grey Owl's articles were reaching a wider public, but money was still scarce. There were times when rations were short indeed at the camp, and the creation of a beaver sanctuary seemed distant. But just when prospects seemed most cheerless, fortune smiled on the naturalist in marvellous manner. Stories concerning Grey Owl and his beaver reached the National Parks Branch in Ottawa at a time when the Branch was especially interested in beaver conservation, and the parks officials determined to learn more about this trapper who had become on his own account a practical conservationist. There could be no doubt of his sincerity or his enthusiasm, and he seemed to be the ideal man for a project which the Branch had formed.

The Branch had enjoyed considerable success with beaver conservation in five parks situated in the Rocky Mountains : some of the engineers might have said that, in one instance, the success was too great, because the beaver in Jasper National Park gained such an affection for their share of that enormous wild-life sanctuary that they tried to halt an important engineering scheme.

It was necessary to lay a pipe-line across a

section of the park, and the work proceeded smoothly until it reached a pool inhabited by beaver. The engineers made a wide gap in the beaver dam, so that they could lay the pipe on the bed of the pool. The beaver saw their water supply rushing away, and took practical steps to prevent further loss. When the men arrived next day to lay the pipe, they found the gap repaired and the dam as solid as before.

Then began a comedy as delightful as any seen on the stage. The men tore a gap in the dam by day, and the animals filled it up again by night. The rapidity with which the beaver worked was amazing, and the humans began to despair : the water could not be drained away while beaver lived in the pool, nor could the animals be touched, because all wild life in the National Parks is rigidly protected by Dominion Statute. The problem was solved by the passing of a special Order by the Dominion Government, permitting the engineers to capture the animals alive and unhurt, and to hand them to the park warden for transfer to another district.

The beaver were popular inmates of Jasper, and, realizing that none would harm them, they

wandered abroad during the daytime. One of
them caused much amusement by hauling a ten-
foot poplar down a bank, across the road and
into a lake. Motorists honked their horns, and
pedestrians laughingly shouted to the furry
worker to " get a move on " : he ignored the
humans and took his time about his business.
When the poplar slid into the water, he posed
himself on a stone, staring at the many on-
lookers who clustered near to photograph him.
Then he plunged into the lake and ferried the
log homewards.

The Parks Branch now wished to form
another beaver sanctuary in a park newly
created in the Riding Mountain district of
Manitoba. It was no difficult task to introduce
the animals to the streams and lakes well
stocked with beaver food, but keeping them
there was another matter. Father Beaver likes
to choose his own settlements, and he can be
extremely stubborn when he chooses. A specialist accustomed to beaver might make the
proposed sanctuary a success, and Grey Owl
had performed wonders with four beaver.
An official of the Branch visited Touladi, saw

the beaver and listened to the ambitious schemes of the naturalist. Grey Owl was offered the appointment as a specialist in the conservation of the beaver and the other animals in Riding Mountain National Park : his courage and sacrifices were rewarded at last.

Rawhide comes for rice

8

THE DREAM COMES TRUE

WITH Grey Owl's appointment to Riding Mountain his fortune was changed indeed. His first book, *Men of the Last Frontier*, brought him immediate recognition as a writer of distinction, critics and public alike welcoming it for its sincerity, freshness and artistry.

Wide publicity for his work followed at once. The Parks Branch sent a battery of cine-cameras to the camp to photograph Grey Owl and his household : Jellyroll and Rawhide were the stars of the film, performing comical but natural actions with excessively solemn faces. Bearing the title of *The Beaver People*, this film has been shown throughout North America and the British Empire, and in many foreign countries, and the behaviour of the two animals has provoked millions of people to hearty laughter, perhaps the funniest incident being the most unladylike manner in which Jellyroll dines on boiled rice. More important is the fact that the film, made possible by the courage and sympathy of Grey Owl, has taught people that wild animals are in some ways very human, and that they have rights and privileges as concrete as those possessed by human beings.

A log cabin was built for Grey Owl at Riding Mountain, and the naturalist transported his family thither. The park was a sanctuary which must have exceeded his wildest dreams : it once formed part of an immense forest reserve, and there is a riotous abundance of spruces, pines, birches, tamarack, ash, elms and maples. Hazel, cranberry and saskatoon bushes abound, and large areas are carpeted with blossoms every summer. Black bears, deer, moose and beaver live in the shady forests, and some three thousand wapiti, the largest herd of wild elk in Canada, roam across its plains. Here also are to be found bison, for twenty of these magnificent creatures were shipped from Buffalo National Park and freed on the rolling plains near Lake Audy. Wild geese, wild ducks, white swan, purple martins, mountain bluebirds, shrikes, juncos and even grosbeaks visit the region—there is a rich variety of animal and bird life, and Grey Owl was to keep a fatherly eye upon all these creatures.

There were, too, sentimental reasons why the naturalist should find the park a desirable place. Less than a century ago, Assiniboine and Cree Indians regarded the Riding Mountain region as their especial territory, but as the bison herds moved westward, the Assiniboines followed them, the Crees remaining as the masters of the district. The lake ridges were Indian highways for countless years, but few red men ascended the mountain to the plateau, believing that the place was full of devils. The white man found much beauty but no devils on this plateau, which is situated 2,200 feet above sea-level : it was a natural, ready-made park before it was made a National Park in 1929. Since that date, conservation and orderly development have made the place a region where men and women can rediscover an enjoyable kinship with their wilder brethren.

Jellyroll and Rawhide liked their new territory, and soon they were plastering mud and laying branches on the dome of a beaver lodge. Those who had argued that National Parks would provide opportunities for studying the minds and the habits of wild animals now found themselves fully justified. Grey Owl gained a friendship with other beaver and a variety of animals, teaching them gradually to lose their mistrust of mankind. He made it possible for students to approach and to observe creatures at close quarters, and even to take motion pictures of them at work and at play amid their natural surroundings. Grey Owl and his animals figured in the films, *The Beaver Family, Strange Doings in Beaverland*, and *Grey Owl's Neighbours*.

Wild stories have been circulated about the beaver's engineering methods, but these films show that he has no cut-and-dried method. Every problem is attacked as it arises, and it is solved by the exercise of common sense. Once, for example, when the animals tried to place a log on the side of the lodge, they found it to be extremely heavy. Instead of abandoning it, they turned it until the narrow end touched the lodge, and took turns to climb on the heavy end, so submerging it and, at the same time, raising the narrow end out of the water.

As the animals plunged into the lake, the pressure of their legs jerked the raised end of the log up the lodge slope. One beaver immediately forced mud under the raised end to wedge it and to prevent any backward slipping of the log. They succeeded in their work by such simple but highly intelligent efforts.

The filmed actions of Jellyroll and Rawhide also killed the legend that beaver plaster mud in position on the dome of the lodge with their tails. Holding their arms laden with mud close to their bodies, they climbed sedately up the slope of the lodge, spilled the material where required, and forced it into position with their hands : they use these limbs so cleverly that it seems silly to call them forepaws. They used their tails as rudders when in the water, to make signals with, as a support when walking erect, and as seats when they squatted to groom their coats, but never as bricklayers' trowels.

They also showed some of the wonderful things which beaver regularly do. One of them would grip a bough of great length and weight, and haul it across the grass, the many-leaved branches swishing against bushes and sweeping up dead leaves. Reaching the water,

he would drag his load afloat, and push it
before him through the water. Getting the
bough ashore was a more difficult task, because
branches became entangled with reeds. The
animal used his wits to save his muscles.
Branches were bitten off and placed in a pile
on the bank for future collection. The bough
was then lifted ashore gradually : the butt end
was hoisted on the grass, then the rest of the
material was raised and placed inshore a few
inches at a time until it was clear of the water.
Then the patient little worker clambered ashore,
set his teeth in the bough, and ran away with it.

The animals cut down saplings with ease and
celerity, but they preferred stealing timber cut
down by men. Fence-poles cut and trimmed
carefully by Grey Owl or the wardens were
regarded as legitimate treasure-trove, and pur-
loined without hesitation.

Beaver reach maturity when two years old,
and normally they begin to breed about six
months later. Baby beaver appeared on the
scene, and the adults watched over them with
great care. Those who denied that animals
educate their young found cause for embarrass-
ment, for the beaver paid close attention to the

schooling of their kittens. The kittens enjoyed a happy care-free existence, wisely and owlishly staring at their parents, noting their actions.

Scrupulously clean animals, the adults kept their coats clean by constant grooming, and the babies tried to copy them. A little bundle of fur but a few weeks old would waddle through the long grasses, tuck his tail between his forelegs and try to sit erect. He would wobble over many times, sometimes forward and sometimes backward, before he gained a balance, then he would squeeze his fur—which was already dry—comb it, brush the tiny moustaches which could just be seen, and smooth the fur on his throat. Without any necessity, he imitated every action made by Rawhide at his toilet : and possibly he thought he was playing a strange and difficult game. In this and in other ways, the kittens copied their parents like so many naughty school children mimicking the school teacher.

There were times when Grey Owl had to assist the beaver by feeding very young kittens with a rubber syringe bulb. The babies would taste the food, then struggle with all their strength to suck as much of it as they could in the shortest possible time, climbing over the man's fingers to reach the bulb. When they could hold no more food, they climbed to his shoulders, found a comfortable place on the neck of his deerskin jacket, and snuggled down to sleep. They had absolute trust in him. That is probably the secret of Grey Owl's success with wild animals. Instead of offering them *his* friendship, he accepted *theirs* : they trusted him, and he never violated it. He wanted them to live naturally, and he refused to force his wishes upon them : they were happy, independent little people regarding him as a reliable elder brother.

The beaver colony prospered, and Grey Owl proceeded to Saskatchewan to undertake similar work at Prince Albert National Park. Jellyroll and Rawhide accompanied him as a matter of course, and quickly settled down at Kingsmere Lake. Their family has increased, and now there are many Jellyrolls and Rawhides ready to answer the call of Grey Owl, although, perhaps, some of the younger animals are not quite as respectful to the naturalist as are the two grandparents.

When young wild beaver are ready to mate,

they travel in search of partners from families other than their own. They return to the colony of the male animal, and the parents may help the young couple to build a lodge for themselves. It will be interesting to see if Grey Owl's " little brothers " will mate with wild female beaver.

Grey Owl's vision of a sanctuary for beaver became a reality at Riding Mountain : it has been duplicated at Kingsmere Lake, but his success has exceeded his wildest dreams. He has taught men to study not only beaver but all wild animals. At Kingsmere Lake he has studied his charges with great fidelity, and recorded his discoveries in sentences of great beauty. In his second book, *Pilgrims of the Wild*, he gave the complete story of his beaver sanctuary from his first vision of it to the triumphant realization of that vision. It is a magnificent story, the chapters dealing with McGinty and McGinnis being especially vivid and moving. The reader feels that the two beaver are people whom he knows intimately, and that he has a personal interest in them. Grey Owl uses the story to illustrate the rights and privileges of animals in no uncertain language, and he makes the reader share his affection and admiration for beaver. With this one book he has made ardent conservationists of many thousands of people whom he will never see.

Some of the incidents described in the story seem utterly impossible, but they are substantiated by film records. When I saw the film, *The Beaver People*, in Ottawa for the first time, I stared in open-mouthed amazement. It was difficult to believe that any man could obtain so close a friendship with the shy and wary beaver. Being well acquainted with beaver, I salute Grey Owl with warm respect and admiration for his great achievement.

A few people find difficulty in accepting Grey Owl as an authority on beaver, and doubt the scientific accuracy of his observations. It is not easy to understand their attitude, because this naturalist has had close contact with beaver since 1928. His books proclaim him to be a man of culture, and the beaver sanctuary expresses his visionary powers. His observations are of living creatures as intimately familiar to him as are the members of his family to the average man : they are therefore bound to differ from the conclusions of those who cling to old ideas, or who study wild life inside museums or from the depths of comfortable armchairs.

Anahareo has played an important part in Grey Owl's work, and he has given her every possible credit for her efforts : she made many sacrifices when times were so difficult that the fate of the sanctuary hung in the balance. She carried on where others would have faltered— Grey Owl's success is her reward.

Although Grey Owl values beaver above all wild creatures, he readily makes friends with other animals and lulls their doubts to rest : while they linger in his sanctuary he embraces every opportunity to study them closely, noting details which most men would consider too trivial to be important. Were he to travel, men and women in many countries would offer him honour and respect : he has chosen the task of watching over his Beaver People, caring more for them than for honours. His work for the beaver has been great, but his efforts for all wild animals have been greater. He has convinced people that conservation is important— that it is as foolish to over-trap animals as it is to withdraw all one's money from the bank and to spend it. As a result, men will now think twice before they hunt any animals during the breeding season.

His work can best be summed up in the National Parks Branch Report for 1934 : " Early in 1931 the National Parks Branch secured the services of Grey Owl, naturalist and writer, best known for his work in the conservation of beaver. Through his association with beaver, Grey Owl assisted in the filming of four of the most remarkable motion pictures ever produced of this enterprising little animal. . . . His articles, and the moving pictures made possible through his co-operation, have done much to impress people with the significance of the conservation of Canada's valuable wild-animal life, and also given prominence to the National Parks of Canada as game sanctuaries."

Centuries ago the Indians respected all animals and conserved the Beaver People. Then came the white man from lands in the east with trinkets and with liquor ; the red man was taught to violate tribal custom and to exploit the creatures of the wilderness. Helping the intruder to amass wealth, the Indian lost his land and his food supplies ; and white men, as the slaves of commerce, slowly harried the animals to extermination over vast areas. Out of the wilderness came Grey Owl in his Indian canoe to teach man conservation, and distracted animals are being given a respite. Trapping will continue while there is a demand for furs, but the public conscience has at last been awakened by Grey Owl: there will be little more callous trapping of animals during the breeding season, and, just in time, the Beaver People have been saved from extinction.

A DESCRIPTION OF THE FALL ACTIVITIES OF BEAVER, WITH SOME REMARKS ON CONSERVATION

By Grey Owl

Reprinted by permission of the National Parks of Canada

WHEN I read of the activities conducted on some fur farms, a feeling of deep regret comes over me to think that any animal as sensitive, sociable and affectionate as a beaver should be so exploited. I can think of few more pitiable sights than that of a domesticated beaver coming to greet his human friend in the perfect confidence of long-established association, to be beaten to death by a heavy club or length of lead piping, the approved method of killing on beaver ranches. A beaver is notoriously hard to kill, and it takes little imagination to conceive the bewilderment, the sudden realization of betrayal, the frenzied fear and despair which in turn enter the brain of the stricken animal during the agonized moments his skull is being crushed in by repeated blows from one he had come to look on as a friend.

Humane methods should always be employed when dealing with wild life, and the two principal objects of conservation kept in mind, which are, firstly, to effect the proper administration of fauna with the minimum of sacrifice of innocent lives, and with due regard to the benefits accruing, not to a few corporations or individuals, but to the many ; secondly, to give intelligent and sympathetic consideration to the claims the animals themselves have on our chivalry and goodwill.

Hunting is the mainstay of our Indian peoples and a few dyed-in-the-wool professional trappers, and the methods followed by these experts are clean and effective. But what chance, we could be excused for conjecturing, has a creed of conservation that puts justice and fair play before individual profit, when we hear of the case of a man of good-nature and kindness of heart, who, owning a fur farm, allowed the aged horses he had bought for feed for his foxes to be crowded into a small corral, while a youth, hired for the purpose, amused himself by practising marksmanship on the poor creatures from an elevation at some distance, afterward coming closer and dispatching the wounded.

I have also in mind the instance of another man who had kept a fox as a pet for some years. This fox had the run of the house and slept in the cellar. He seemed to have thought a lot of the beast and had taught it some tricks, such as getting his rubbers and other such performances. His wife used to show great affection for this much-loved pet, even allowing it to take chocolates from between her lips. The man himself on one occasion had spent part of a night out in the snow-bound woods retrieving the animal, who, helpless in his natural but unaccustomed environment, had been lost. I had entertained a rather high regard for this man, but he lost a little of that when I learned that he had allowed the poor little beast to be shot, using the fur for an ornament for his wife.

Facts such as these that have come to my notice at first hand, together with the realization of the utter disregard by man of the rights of any living creature save himself, are what caused me to take up the cudgels in defence of wild life in general, and particularly on the part of the beaver, which is easily the most sensitive and sagacious of our North American mammals.

I am doing my utmost to disseminate knowledge concerning our national animal, the beaver, in the hope of eventually gaining for him a recognition and an immunity from brutality, which I have by close observation of his qualities come to consider his due. Yet I am careful not to divulge any information which would betray him into the hands of the greedy, the thoughtless, or the unscrupulous.

My own colony is safely expanding under the protection of the National Parks of Canada, a branch of the Dominion Government, and this places the inhabitants for all time beyond the reach of hungry men of commerce. It affords a great deal of satisfaction to know that where beaver culture is engaged in from a business standpoint the difficulties encountered are such that its scope must be very limited.

In my former life as a trapper a certain amount of data concerning the habits and history of the various animals was accumulated as a matter of course. I had thought my knowledge to be fairly comprehensive after years spent on the trail, but later and more intimate association with some of these animals has taught me my error, and I now begin to see how inadequate my education in wild life subjects has been. To-day, after five years of the closest observation of wild life under ideal conditions, I am no longer surprised when some new and unexpected trait manifests itself in my animal friends, as when I discover that a moose is as well able to follow a blazed trail as I, or that some line of action which I have after long experience and considerable thinking figured out for myself, is old stuff to the beaver.

The beaver accomplishes practically all his work and overcomes his numerous difficulties with no spectacular display of quick-witted subtlety. His sagacity is more of the calculating kind ; he is long-headed, and ensures the success of his operations by elaborate preparations and plans painstakingly carried out. Where his strength does not suffice, he gains his ends by strategy. The ingenious devices by which he overcomes apparently insurmountable obstacles, the studied economy of his movements, his ability to take advantage of the means at hand,

and his perseverance in the face of adverse conditions must compel the respect of even the casual observer. What cannot be pulled may be pushed ; sticks he finds impossible to lift, he rolls. His patience is such that in the event of a tree being lodged in an almost perpendicular position, he will cut it off again, allowing the trunk thus to drop down a length. If it does not then fall, he will sometimes take off another cut, and another, if the tree be especially desirable, or feed scarce, until the entangled limbs are clear of the obstruction and the tree falls. In this operation he is not always successful, but he has the fortitude to attempt it.

The beaver wastes little of his materials and makes few mistakes. His skilful manipulation of awkward loads and large size sticks, and his ability to distinguish the line of least resistance and to follow it, enable him to operate under the most adverse conditions.

Although these powerful animals can work at top speed and accomplish a vast amount in a short time if hard pressed, they are generally very deliberate in their movements, depending not so much on speed as accuracy. Before felling timber in dangerous situations they examine carefully the terrain at its foot, removing obstacles that would interfere with their footing at the base of the tree, and make all arrangements for a quick get-away. They size up the lean of the tree, and cut deeply on the side it should go, trim the sides after and finally sever it from behind. Although they are able to arrange their cutting in accordance with the probable fall of the tree they want, they are unable to judge the effect of obstacles standing some distance away, such as other timber which may intercept their tree and lodge it. Trees thus hung up, if efforts to dislodge them finally prove ineffective, are left severely alone. Long before the movement of the tree can be detected by the eye, they appear to receive ample warning to stand clear, which I believe to be given by the action of the fibres in the core and sensed by the teeth. Given a sufficient grade on which to gather speed, the beaver will race the falling tree to the water, even if it should be dropping directly into the runway. So accurate are their calculations that they are never caught, although they take no such chances when felling big timber, in which case they retire a few yards in the proper direction to ensure safety. Even a log that jumps the stump and ploughs deeply into the ground they easily avoid, and when a log falls which has been suspended horizontally—for in their cuttings timber lies criss-crossed at every imaginable angle—they can snap away from beneath with the quick dart of a striking rattlesnake. They work at a high nervous tension at such times, and attempts to safeguard them against possible accident only result in upsetting their calculations and imperilling their safety. Once, when I was standing too close to a female beaver and the tree was about to fall, she came over to me and tried to push me away from what subsequently turned out to be her prearranged line of retreat.

In spite of their ponderous build, short legs and awkward appearance, they escape scathless from some very hazardous situations, not so much as the result of any agility they may possess, but owing to careful manœuvring for position, and a careful attention to detail in respect of the preparations made to ensure a clear retreat. I seldom meddle in their business on these dangerous occasions, as my presence at such times causes uneasiness which sometimes evinces itself in muttered protest on the part of Jellyroll, the female, or the discontinuance of his labours of the more methodical Rawhide. This Rawhide, the male and father of the family, is much given to working apart from the others, and this self-abnegation is characteristic of most heads of beaver colonies. Although he takes kindly to domestication, and has, in his quiet unobtrusive way, adapted himself very thoroughly to camp life, he retains nearly all the characteristics of a wild beaver so far as his work is concerned, and will not tolerate any of my offers of help, hoeing his own row with diligent persistence.

Jellyroll, however, accepts my occasional co-operation as her right, sometimes seeming to expect it ; but instead of taking advantage of it as a fair division of labour, she sees her chance to get that much more work done, and attempts to haul sticks of timber or move loads that are more than enough for the two of us, attacking the project with an impetuous violence which I am supposed, apparently, to emulate. She is pretty shrewd and misses no bets, being an opportunist of the first water, and belongs to that rare type of worker who finds the day all too short for his purpose. Although highly to be commended for her industry, she will break off from her work almost any time to play, if she sees the canoe passing. She is also very self-assertive, and has no intention of being overlooked when there is any company around, or anything especially good to eat to be had.

While beaver will work together on the larger tasks such as house and dam building and the formation of a feed-raft, they have no idea of co-operating to the extent of assisting one another. Each works independent of the other, except in rare instances, even if all hands are engaged on the same task. Any member of a family will make use of runways and other works prepared by his companions, and will cut and haul away a tree felled by some one else if it is not soon dealt with by its owner. But any work so stolen is, like all the rest of their activities, done for the general good. These observations, however, do not apply to the young beaver of up to three or four months of age. During late fall they commence to perform some useful work, but up to that time few of the rules which govern adult beaver behaviour seem to apply to the kittens. They lead a happy care-free existence of playing, wrestling, and exploring. They roam the waters of the home pond in pairs or groups, and seem much attached to one another, signalling with shrill cries when separated. They pester the older beaver at their work, and although this must be very exasperating, the adults show no signs of irritation, and will go to a great deal of trouble to avoid injuring them accidentally. This is difficult as the little fellows seem to be always in the way of a heavy log or under a pile of limbs, or crowded together at the foot of a runway. They seem to be protected by the good luck that favours all irresponsibles, and come out of every jam unhurt and looking for more excitement.

The passage near any group of them of a large beaver with a tow, is to them a heaven-sent opportunity for excitement. With a concerted rush they attack the convoy, attaching themselves to the load, pulling at it, cutting pieces off it, climbing on the laden animal's back, or vainly trying to engage him in a wrestling match, or some other aquatic sport. Such diversions serve to break the monotony of life on a small pond, but are a serious matter for

Jellyroll at work

the harassed object of this persecution, who takes it all in good part, although he or she is not above resorting to such subterfuges as waiting motionless until the band of marauders disperse, or diving suddenly and swimming beneath the surface to dislodge them. But these stratagems seldom succeed, as at the first movement, or in the latter case, on his reappearance from the depths, the parasitic little demons descend on him and pursue him until he has disposed of his load. A procession of this description with its varied and tumultuous movement, with attendant uproar, adds a gay and carnival-like air to the otherwise somewhat sober proceedings, but must take a considerable toll in energy and patience.

The lively scuffling and tussling in which the kittens engage amongst themselves is often quite rough though harmless. There is always one of their number who considers himself a match for two or three others, and some day inevitably gets himself set upon by the entire crowd of youngsters. If this occurs on land where escape is difficult he is quickly disillusioned of his vaunted prowess. Unable to stand the pressure he will eventually make a dash for the water, and throw himself in on head, back, side, or whichever part arrives first and sink like a stone out of sight. The incident seems to be soon forgotten, as these little animals take nothing very seriously, and the deposed champion on his return is not further molested.

Beaver generate in their sturdy bodies a resistless energy and a power of endurance which enables them to carry on labours little short of marvellous, for long periods at a time without fatigue. Once this nervous force is exhausted, they relax utterly and do little except sleep, as in winter, meanwhile storing up fresh resources for the future. They seldom rest if actively engaged in serious business, but change from one job to another, not working more than an hour or so at one task, seeming to find, as do humans, that a change is as good as a rest.

Beaver make full use of any materials at hand, and some of their arrangements are made to serve two or more purposes. They dredge out the bottom of the lake under their feed pile to deepen the water before the entrance tunnel, and to accommodate the ever-increasing cache of supplies, using the mud so displaced in a further strengthening of the walls of the house.

Peeled sticks, discarded feed and debris from off the runways are added to the structure of house or dam. The well-known feed-raft is not only a larder containing six months' supplies, but it acts also as a breakwater that keeps down the agitation of the water in the plunge-hole during stormy weather, avoiding the undue wetting of the interior of the house. It also forms a protecting mat under which the tiny kittens in their earlier stages may take shelter if alarmed or attacked by predatory birds, a common enough occurrence ; and there is always a placid area of still water between one projecting wing of the raft and the shore line, where the helpless little creatures can disport themselves as in a harbour.

As fall approaches, this mesh of limbs, saplings and brush is added to and woven tighter and tighter ; heavy logs are laid on it, and it gradually submerges until little of it remains above the surface. Whatever part of it freezes in, remains in cold storage all winter, to be eaten in late March or April as it thaws out of the ice, by which time the residue of the feed that has remained in the water during the cold months has soured. The ice is kept thinned down around the feed by the creation of a layer of air bubbles under its surface, and by the movements of the beaver especially in channels they may use frequently. In some instances, as when the family be large, there is practically no ice before the lodge, just enough to support a layer of snow, and I know of a trapper who broke through in such a spot and was drowned in front of the beaver house.

The bulk of the feed, including all the choicer portions, is taken bodily under the raft, and one end is pushed up into it in such a manner as to be easily liberated by a downward pull, when needed, the stick being in a perpendicular position. A hook formed by a limb cut short is frequently used to attach short bulky cuts to the under side, but many of the longer portions stand erect with the upper end enmeshed in the mat of brush above it, and are visible below the surface to an observer in a canoe, and sometimes can be seen from the shore.

This device has given rise to the fiction that beaver are capable of causing sticks to float upright under the water, by means of some mysterious power they are gifted with. They have no such ability, save as above described. This erroneous idea probably gained credence on account of the tendency of water-logged poplar poles to float in this position, with the heavy end down, of their own accord. This belief is only one of the widely spread but entirely unfounded superstitions with regard to beaver that have been circulated by those who should have been more sure of their facts. One writer in a well-known magazine wrote an interesting and highly imaginative article on beaver, in which amongst other absurdities he claimed that he *saw a beaver blow a bubble on the end of a stick*, dig a hole in the soft muskeg soil of the lake bottom, place one end of the stick in the hole *with the bubble still on it* and *tamp it down with his hind feet and tail*. Without troubling to contradict the fore part of this legend, let me point out with regard to the rest of it, that a beaver is incapable of standing erect under water to tamp anything down, and cannot even remain on all fours on the bottom of still water as his rear end floats up on him unless he be in motion ; the only time he can walk along the bottom is in swift water and then only up-stream. He uses this method to climb a rapids. The beaver never uses his tail for any tamping, trowelling, digging or lifting of any material whatsoever, and the few occasional short slaps he gives with it as he works on a lodge are to keep him from slipping on the greasy mud. He will, if enraged and about to attack an adversary, thump heavily with his tail on the ground—this however is a very rare occurrence. He employs this broad rubbery looking appendage in several distinctly different ways. It serves as a rudder and, under some circumstances, as when making a quick get-away in shallow water, as a sculling oar or propeller.

By forcing backward and upward with the flat of his tail against the water and simultaneously surging ahead with the body, logs can be driven into a desired position and firmly embedded or shoved up on to an elevation. With it he gains leverage in hauling or moving heavy materials both on land and water. On shore or on the sides of the lodge it serves as a prop while he carries his loads in an erect position; in this attitude he can walk forty or fifty feet, and the energy required to portage in his arms a load of mud, sticks and stones up the slippery and uneven sides of a beaver house, is equivalent almost to that which would be expended by a man carrying a bag of flour before him up the roof of a barn. This much discussed and indispensable tail makes for him a very effective balancing pole as he walks on a log, and if he is working clear of the ground he uses it as a support by pressing the end of it firmly against the ground. The final and better-known use of it as a signalling apparatus needs little comment, save that its resounding smack is not only a danger signal, but with variations perceptible to the ears of the initiated, is a means of communication, such as giving notice of the owner's approach or whereabouts, as an answer to a call, as a challenge, and as a means of attracting desired attention.

Beaver appear to experience no difficulty in cutting frozen timber, but must have frequent recourse to water in temperature much below freezing to keep the unprotected tail from becoming frost-bitten.

This fall, whilst the ice was making, the entire family were busy breaking and thinning it down in the vicinity of the bank, dens and house, for they will not permit the ice to thicken over the approaches to these retreats, so that they may be serviceable in cases of emergency. Although the ice was all of four inches thick over the rest of the lake and daily becoming thicker, they succeeded in maintaining a channel of open water along the shore nearly fifty yards in length; and of a width that would have accommodated two canoes abreast. Every night this became frozen over, but early the following afternoon they would be all out breaking the new scum. Ice half an inch in thickness would be broken from below in several places, and the areas between the holes broken down with the forepaws. Any heavier ice was heaved up with the head and shoulders, the powerful tail being propelled vigorously against the water to obtain the necessary leverage, so that the ice was forced upward in long narrow ridges. At some point where it was shattered sufficiently, the beaver gnawed a hole and climbing out on to the heaved-up portions with little difficulty broke them down. Ice that does not rest on water is as brittle as glass, and will support little weight, buckling easily under the pressure of a hundred or so pounds. The slabs that remain are broken up and carried or driven under the heavy ice on the deep-water side, where they remain safely out of the way. Floating fragments thus removed, the ragged edges at landing-places are bitten off smooth. Ice of over an inch thickness can be disposed of in this manner, and in the canal thus formed the work of hauling and towing goes on uninterruptedly, whilst alongside is the natural ice on which a moose could walk in safety.

This watery highway eventually froze up during more severe weather, and Jellyroll then took to frequenting the water hole after it was opened for our own purposes, and through it I fed her quantities of apples. She took away a large supply on each visit, and on her return home the sounds of strife, followed by a steady and contented munching and grunts of contentment in different keys, gave evidence of her generosity to those who made up in appetite what they lacked in enterprise. I surmise that air that is very frosty must cause discomfort to lungs acclimatized to soft weather and the humid atmosphere of a beaver house. I was led to believe this by the fact that in cold weather Jellyroll never emitted any of her usual welcoming notes when her head appeared above the water, and closer inspection revealed that she never drew breath while in the open, which accounts for her hurried withdrawals. These excursions are unnatural to her in really cold weather and I do not encourage them for fear of causing complications which her precautions leave me to think she fears. I now allow a new scum of ice to form on the water hole and when it is sufficiently thick to retain them, I shove the apples in under it. Thus submerged they do not freeze, and she is no longer obliged to be exposed to the cold air. So I do not see her, but the apples disappear with monotonous regularity.

Out on the frozen frontage of my cabin stands another beaver house, a replica of the one indoors. It is at present empty. No doubt it will be put to use next spring, according to some plan they must have, of which I anxiously await the fulfilment. This house to let is a pretty bleak and lonesome-looking erection and emanates all the cold hostility that surrounds a house whose owners have decided to be not at home, and I at times feel rebuffed as I look at it in the pale glow o' the Northern lights.

On entering the cabin and hailing the invisible company who occupy the lodge that stands within it, I get a lazy mumbled answer to my call. I hear also a few whimpers of protest from bedfellows who enter sleepily into the age-old discussion as to who has all the bed.

Sounds of slumber issue from the bowels of the thick-walled lodge, as some tired worker rolls over on his back and snores prodigiously in the security he has worked so hard to earn, whilst he dreams, perhaps, of lake shores lined with apples.

And I know that all is well with my Beaver People, and that I also may now call it the end of a day.

Grey Owl in his cabin

NOTES

FACTS CONCERNING BEAVER LIFE ESTABLISHED BY GREY OWL

1. That they can and do select, where possible, trees that will fall towards the water.

2. That they notch the tree in accordance with the proposed fall of the tree.

3. That they have no power to ascertain if a tree will be lodged, even if they decide accurately the direction of its fall.

4. That they can detect by means of the pressure and movement of fibres the imminent falling of a tree before it can be detected by the eye, and having knowledge of the direction it will fall in, will move aside to safety, or in the case of small trees falling into the runway, race to the water before the trees fall.

5. That large and dangerous trees are often severed nearly through and kept clear of until they fall naturally or are blown down.

6. That in their present state of freedom, domesticity has not in any way impaired the knowledge of their work, nor has it lessened their ability to detect the presence of immediate danger.

7. That they are able to recognize my step, voice and movements.

8. That their confidence in one man (at a time, presumably) is such that in running at full speed to the water from some danger, a word will check them, even at the water's edge, and they can be easily reassured.

9. That they have a very strong affection for each other and one or two humans.

10. That they have a long memory, or apparently no idea of the passage of time, as they will pick up work where it was laid down weeks before, and long absence does not lessen their recognition of places and well-known persons.

11. That they can recognize at least two colours, red, which they like, and white which they do not.

12. That they are able to pick almost un-erringly the most advantageous places for dams and other works.

13. That they do actually conserve water for their own uses, damming besides the outlet, every creek coming into their lake, or most of them, sometimes in a series of dams farther and farther up-stream. In the event of loss of water in the pond through damage to main dam, the dam is repaired and the upper reservoirs are then broken and allowed to flow into the pond.

14. That they breed not in March or February, as supposed, but in fall, the exact date I am unable as yet to determine.

15. That the male helps to care for the young, takes an intelligent interest in their welfare, and has as much affection for them as the mother has.

CANADA'S WILD LIFE SANCTUARIES

Census estimate of December 31, 1931

IN ALBERTA :

Banff National Park (2,585 sq. miles). Black
bears, grizzly bears, beaver (400), mule
deer, wapiti, moose, muskrats, Rocky
Mountain goats, R. M. sheep.

Jasper National Park (4,200 sq. miles). Grizzly
bears, black bears (4,000), beaver (100),
caribou (10,000), white-tailed deer
(22,000), wapiti, moose (10,000), R. M.
goat (7,000), R. M. sheep (22,000).

Waterton Lakes National Park (220 sq. miles).
Black bear, beaver (1,000), mule deer
(1,050), wapiti, R. M. goat, R. M. sheep.

Buffalo National Park (197.5 sq. miles). Bison
(6,000), mule deer (2,000), wapiti, moose,
yak.

Nemiskam National Park (85 sq. miles). Pronghorn antelope.

IN BRITISH COLUMBIA :

Glacier National Park (521 sq. miles). Bear, caribou, deer, R. M. goat.

Kootenay National Park (587 sq. miles). Bear, beaver (150), coyote, deer, wapiti, fox, lynx, marten, mink, moose, otter, R. M. goat, R. M. sheep, weasel, wolverine.

IN MANITOBA :

Riding Mountain National Park (1,148 sq. miles). Bear, beaver (75), white-tailed deer, wapiti (2,000), moose, muskrat, otter.

IN SASKATCHEWAN :

Prince Albert National Park (1,869 sq. miles). Bear, beaver, caribou, coyote, white-tailed deer (3,500), wapiti (1,000), moose (2,500), wolf.

Total area of all the National Parks, excluding the Wood Buffalo Reserve= 12,059 sq. miles.

PRINTED IN GREAT BRITAIN AT
THE PRESS OF THE PUBLISHERS

A SEASHORE CALENDAR

L. R. BRIGHTWELL, F.Z.S.

With 70 illustrations by the author

A chronicle of the sea and the seashore, month by month, "Delightfully told and clearly illustrated. The stories of the herring, salmon, eel, and whale vie with those of the oyster and the shrimp in holding our attention. We watch the guillemot push its baby over a two-hundred-foot cliff into the sea, and read of the worm called bootlaces, that may be cut into twenty pieces, each of which can grow a new head and tail . . ."—*Time and Tide.* "A vast amount of accurate information."—*Times Literary Supplement.* "I'd have you buy it."—*Punch.* *Cloth gilt, 6s. net.*

THE KINDRED OF THE WILD
HAUNTERS OF THE SILENCES
WATCHERS OF THE TRAILS

by SIR CHARLES G. D. ROBERTS

These three volumes, by the famous Canadian author who has just been knighted, contain short stories of wild life which are among the best ever written. They are proving more popular than ever in these cheap editions. (Edinburgh Library.) *Cloth gilt, each 2s. 6d. net.* " Haunters of the Silences " is issued also in a special edition, beautifully illustrated in colour and line by Stuart Tresilian, at 3s. 6d. net.

WILD LIFE STUDIES

by FRANCES PITT

Illustrated by G. E. Collins

These twenty studies, by a famous naturalist, are
written with charm and understanding as well
as knowledge. They give us fascinating pictures of the lives of badgers, kestrels, dormice,
grey seals, owls, puffins, and other creatures of
the English wild, and they are illustrated from
exquisite pen-drawings by a distinguished etcher.
(Argosy Books.)   *Cloth gilt,* 3s. 6d. *net.*